I0407960

Editor-in-Chief and Founder:
 Lyndon H. LaRouche, Jr.
Editorial Board: *Lyndon H. LaRouche, Jr. , Helga
 Zepp-LaRouche, Robert Ingraham, Tony
 Papert, Gerald Rose, Dennis Small, Jeffrey
 Steinberg, William Wertz*
Co-Editors: *Robert Ingraham, Tony Papert*
Managing Editor: *Nancy Spannaus*
Technology: *Marsha Freeman*
Books: *Katherine Notley*
Ebooks: *Richard Burden*
Graphics: *Alan Yue*
Photos: *Stuart Lewis*
Circulation Manager: *Stanley Ezrol*

INTELLIGENCE DIRECTORS
Counterintelligence: *Jeffrey Steinberg, Michele
 Steinberg*
Economics: *John Hoefle, Marcia Merry Baker,
 Paul Gallagher*
History: *Anton Chaitkin*
Ibero-America: *Dennis Small*
Russia and Eastern Europe: *Rachel Douglas*
United States: *Debra Freeman*

INTERNATIONAL BUREAUS
Bogotá: *Miriam Redondo*
Berlin: *Rainer Apel*
Copenhagen: *Tom Gillesberg*
Houston: *Harley Schlanger*
Lima: *Sara Madueño*
Melbourne: *Robert Barwick*
Mexico City: *Gerardo Castilleja Chávez*
New Delhi: *Ramtanu Maitra*
Paris: *Christine Bierre*
Stockholm: *Ulf Sandmark*
United Nations, N.Y.C.: *Leni Rubinstein*
Washington, D.C.: *William Jones*
Wiesbaden: *Göran Haglund*

ON THE WEB
e-mail: eirns@larouchepub.com
www.larouchepub.com
www.executiveintelligencereview.com
www.larouchepub.com/eiw
Webmaster: *John Sigerson*
Assistant Webmaster: *George Hollis*
Editor, Arabic-language edition: *Hussein Askary*

EIR (ISSN 0273-6314) *is published weekly
(50 issues), by EIR News Service, Inc.,
P.O. Box 17390, Washington, D.C. 20041-0390.
(703) 777-9451 ext. 415*

European Headquarters: E.I.R. GmbH, Postfach
Bahnstrasse 9a, D-65205, Wiesbaden, Germany
Tel: 49-611-73650
Homepage: http://www.eirna.com
e-mail: eirna@eirna.com
Director: Georg Neudecker

Montreal, Canada: 514-461-1557

Denmark: EIR - Danmark, Sankt Knuds Vej 11,
basement left, DK-1903 Frederiksberg, Denmark.
Tel.: +45 35 43 60 40, Fax: +45 35 43 87 57. e-mail:
eirdk@hotmail.com.

Mexico City: EIR, Sor Juana Inés de la Cruz 242-2
Col. Agricultura C.P. 11360
Delegación M. Hidalgo, México D.F.
Tel. (5525) 5318-2301
eirmexico@gmail.com

Canada Post Publication Sales Agreement
#40683579

Postmaster: Send all address changes to *EIR*, P.O.
Box 17390, Washington, D.C. 20041-0390.

Signed articles in *EIR* represent the views of the
authors, and not necessarily those of the Editorial
Board.

Shut Obama Down

EDITORIAL

The Denial of Reality by Narcissistic 'Democrats' Takes on Clinical Dimensions

by Helga Zepp-LaRouche

Feb. 25—The collective hysteria seizing the neoliberal, vulture globalist trans-Atlantic Establishment—in the face of far-reaching strategic changes manifest in the Trump Presidency and the New Silk Road dynamic—represents a new kind of mass-psychological phenomenon. In a symbiotic conflation of group-think and group-narcissism, these advocates of the oh-so-democratic "western community of values" indulge in diatribes of the basest sort against those who think otherwise, so much so that it doesn't even occur to them that they are acting dictatorially.

The most dramatic example of this clinical loss of touch with reality is surely the pathological excitement with which every statement by President Trump is commented upon. A recent example is Trump's Feb. 24 speech at the Conservative Political Action Conference at National Harbor in Maryland. He pointed out the obvious, that the United States has spent six trillion dollars or more over the last fifteen years for wars in the Middle East and Libya, and the region is much the worse for it today. If the former presidents had instead gone to the beach during that time, we would all be much better off today, he said, and added that we could have rebuilt our country three times over with that money.

But the media found these views unworthy of comment, and instead hyperventilated over the fact that several of their number, who had previously distinguished themselves with particularly vicious reporting against Trump, were not invited to be part of the White House media pool. And where were these media and their co-thinker politicians, when the Bush and Obama governments—supported by the same "western community of values"—were bombing countries in the Middle East for years, and arming terrorist groups, actions which cost more than a million lives and brought unspeakable suffering to many millions of families, without which the refugee crisis would not have erupted as it has?

Did they simply oppose Trump's demand that Europe must spend more money for rearmament—because there is no threat, there is no Warsaw Pact any more, and Russia has no plans for conquest, neither of the Baltic states, or Poland, or anywhere else, while NATO and the European Union (EU) have expanded right up to Russia's borders? No. These media are reacting no less hysterically with demands for the nuclear rearmament of Germany and the European Union. "Does the EU Need the Bomb?" wrote co-authors Peter Dausend and Michael Thumann of the oh-so-liberal *Zeit* recently; they thus betrayed where the real warmongers reside—namely, in the editorial offices of their newspaper.

The neoliberal, neoconservative Establishment just can't manage to analyze the failure of its paradigm and correct it accordingly.

Sabotaging the Silk Road

Another example of the absurdity of this behavior is the most recent EU action against the Chinese-financed stretch of high-speed rail between Belgrade and Budapest. This 350 kilometer rail segment, first proposed by President Xi Jinping in 2013, will reduce travel time between the two capitals from 8 to 3 hours and will obviously be very beneficial for the countries concerned, Serbia and Hungary, as well as for the entire Balkan region. But the EU has now launched an investigation into whether the project will pay for itself (!) and whether it conforms to EU guidelines. Yet Serbia is not even a member of the EU!

The people of the Balkan states are painfully aware that the EU has not built a single one of the transport corridors originally decided upon at the conference of EU Transport Ministers in 1994 in Crete, but which then fell victim to the austerity policy of the EU Commission and the European Central Bank. So no one should be surprised that the Central and Eastern European countries, and the Balkan countries, see their future in the expansion of the New Silk Road, China's Belt and Road Initiative, which opens to them the prospect of participating in the most dynamic and most gigantic infrastructure projects the world has ever seen. Instead of responding positively to China's many offers of cooperation and seizing the enormous economic opportunities which lie in the win-win cooperation of all of Eurasia, the neoliberal EU bureaucracy is attempting, from a position of weakness, to exert a control which it has long since lost, as the desolate situation of the EU shows.

China's *Global Times* wrote this about the EU action on Feb. 23: "The EU is experiencing a tough time and may seek to assert its authority by ramping up inspections and reviews, but the EU may have hit a dead end. It is unknown whose interest the EU's investigation represents." Nevertheless, it added, China will try to persuade the EU of the advantages of cooperation.

Less dim-witted is PricewaterhouseCoopers (PwC), the world's second largest accounting firm, which is based in London and operates in 152 countries, with 756 subsidiaries and 223,000 employees. It published a comprehensive overview under its rubric, "PwC B&R Watch," under the headline: "China and Belt & Road Infrastructure: 2016 Review and Outlook" (February 2017), in which, with the aid of many maps and illustrations, it demonstrates the enormous potential of China's Belt and Road Initiative. The Initiative already involves three continents and 66 countries, and stretches from Lithuania to Indonesia, it notes; all have profited from explosive growth, which is bringing enormous benefits in transportation, energy production, communications, health care, and many other areas.

The EU's strange attitude has long since become a subject of discussion in Asia. The S. Rajaratnam School of International Studies in Singapore raised the question almost a year ago as to whether the EU had already missed the train of the New Silk Road. The European media have focused exclusively on Chinese takeovers, it noted, while entirely neglecting to explain the enormous potential that cooperation with China would bring to all sides. As a result, Europe's citizens are extremely poorly informed.

Evil Humor

Even though the famous annual carnival program in Mainz is not as important as one or another of its proponents might think, this year's version lends itself well to demonstrating the evil character of the group narcissism of the Establishment, which was at least selectively gathered in the audience. Several of the skits, such as those of Hans-Peter Betz and Lars Reichow, for example, had nothing to do with humor, being simply poisonous insults of the lowest level against Trump, to which—judging from the camera work—the audience responded with approval.

These skits not only betrayed bad taste, but reflect a hostility that shows how fragile the political situation is, and how flimsy the façade of the "western community of values" has become. Behind this façade we find that same claim to being the sole legitimate authority—a link to the unipolar world order—that meant there were no demonstrations against the wars based on lies in the Middle East. It is for precisely this reason that the neoliberal neocons are whining for the "nice" Obama. And it is less likely that Trump would have a problem finding Germany on the map— as one of the so-called comics claimed—than that they themselves would have trouble locating Yemen.

The world will continue to change dramatically over the next months, just as we have seen it do over the last year. If we are lucky, it will turn out the way it did the last time a system came to an end: There will be many about-faces and some people will keep on being blockheads. The difference is that this time, a large majority of countries is ready to set up an entirely new kind of cooperation among nation-states. The nations of Europe have the choice of either cooperating for a common destiny for the future of mankind, or soon be among the "also-rans."

EIRContents

www.larouchepub.com Volume 44, Number 9, March 3, 2017

Cover This Week

Predator drone with hellfire missiles.

Corrections
In "Musical Dialogue-of-Culture Concert Breakthrough in Copenhagen" by Michelle Rasmussen, in our Feb. 24 issue, pages 36-38, please note these corrections: The concert was held in The Russian Center for Science and Culture, representing the Federal agency for the Commonwealth of Independent States (of the former Soviet Union) for compatriots living abroad and for international humanistic cooperation (*Rossotrudnichestvo*). The China Culture Center in Denmark is independent of the Embassy of China. The musician Kai Guo is from China's Inner Mongolia region. The photo of soloist Leena Malkki is a video screenshot. Anika Telmányi Lylloff's and Benjamin Telmányi Lylloff's ancestor was Emil Telmányi.

I. The Eurasia Strategy

LAUNCH A RENAISSANCE!

The Belt and Road Summit Is the Platform

by Michael G. Steger

Feb. 27—During the first decades of the 15th Century, in the area of Florence, Italy, a rather small number of creative geniuses launched what became known as the Italian Renaissance. The Renaissance, as we refer to this period of transformative beauty and scientific development, touched every area of human society for centuries to come: e.g. medicine, painting, poetry and music—technology itself was born in the hands of Brunelleschi and his cupola, even the exploration to the new world, and the first principles of statecraft by Nicholas of Cusa, and an explosion of self-conscious creative thought that continued to foster scientific revolutions for hundreds of years to come, including even the founding of the U.S. Constitutional System and the American System of Economics by Alexander Hamilton.

This Renaissance, which changed the course of human history, did not happen to this small set of creative leaders, and it was not, as many might imagine, an inevitability. But why would earlier periods of development, as with Charlemagne or the Cathedral building as in Chartres, not become a Renaissance, not become the explosion of creative thought and an outpouring of new and successful ideas that became the Florentine Renaissance?

These lesser periods can be characterized by an insufficient knowledge and courage to overcome the culturally-intrinsic boundary of human identity at that time; a boundary, to be more specific, which is self-bounded by the socially-accepted notions of human creativity itself. What was required, was a demonstration and development of an entirely new and higher conception of human identity.

And so the Renaissance occurred, as with Brunelleschi's cupola, created from the voluntary and impassioned

actions of a small number of creative figures intending to do just that.[1] And as if out of the blue, and by its effects, European Civilization emerged once and for all free from the confines of the Middle Ages, and began what was to become, over the last 600 years, the greatest period of human development that mankind has ever seen.[2]

The Belt and Road to the Future

On May 14 and 15 of 2017, China will host a major international summit on the "One Belt One Road" Initiative in the capital city of Beijing, a program President Xi Jinping launched in September and November of 2013.[3] Invitations have presumably gone out to every head of state of every nation, and the Chinese are modestly expecting 30 heads of state, while it remains likely that many more will attend. Nations from nearly every continent have already accepted, including Great Britain, Switzerland, Tunisia, Russia, Sri Lanka, and Chile. One can expect many of the nations directly involved in the current One Belt One Road (OBOR) projects, such

---

1. Those familiar with the Council of Florence held at the Santa María del Fiore of Brunelleschi's cupola in 1439, will quickly see the parallels between that decisive point, and the upcoming summit today.

2. Consider the population growth chart, which irrefutably shows the qualitative leap in human economy and standard of living which stemmed from the revolutionary upshift in science, statecraft and culture of the Italian Renaissance.

3. It is not a coincidence that the Ukraine Coup, supported by Obama's State Department and controlled by Neo-Nazi organizations in Ukraine, was launched at this same time. Former leaders of Ukraine have stated that the protests, which provided a cover for the coup, were actually planned for 2015. Was the British and Obama time table pushed forward by the threat of this new economic paradigm? Were they again threatening another world war, this time nuclear? Such has been the story of our past century.

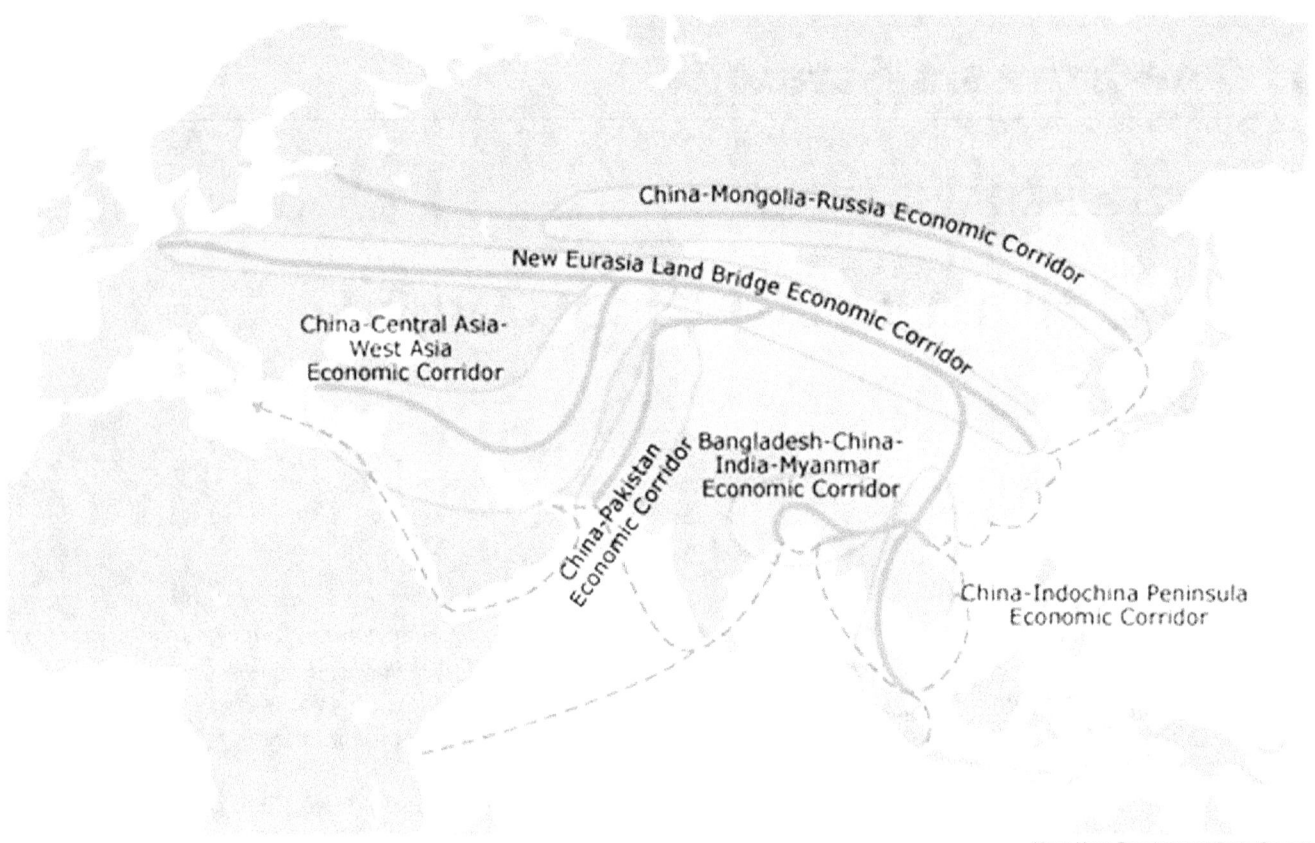

The Belt and Road Initiative: six economic corridors spanning Asia, Europe, and Africa.

as Ethiopia, Pakistan, and Iran, plus the nations of central and southeast Asia, will also be in attendance, making this the largest and most significant assembly of heads of state of nations, regarding global economic development, since the Non-Aligned Movement's meeting in Colombo, Sri Lanka in 1976.

However, with major trans-Atlantic nations potentially attending this Belt and Road Summit, including possibly even the United States, the only comparison to such an event, for the modern era, is the Bretton Woods Conference of 1944, held by President Franklin Roosevelt in Bretton Woods, New Hampshire, to set the foundations for the post-war paradigm's new international system. Unfortunately, President Roosevelt's post-war vision of economic development was not fulfilled, and within 25 years, by 1971, the system he established to raise the former colonial nations out of their colonial past, was tossed aside and replaced with a Wall Street and London-dominated system set to loot the developing world, and eventually, as we see today, even the developed world, simply to keep their system alive.

Now as the British-Wall Street system perishes,

dying under the weight of the revolts of citizens across the trans-Atlantic region, we are left to resolve the crucial paradox—either we confront the intrinsic boundary which had ultimately predetermined this system's inevitable failure, or the new system, which we are now constructing, will also eventually fail.

Consider FDR's Post-War Vision

When Elliott Roosevelt, the son of President Roosevelt, wrote his book, *As He Saw It,* in 1946, the system envisioned by his father was already becoming undone by Churchill and Truman's Cold War ideological warfare.

In the Cairo Conference of 1943, FDR promised Chiang Kai-shek, the Nationalist President of the Republic of China, that following the war, there would be no British ships in Chinese ports. With the untimely death of President Roosevelt, this promise was quickly broken.

Though there were many other mistakes in U.S. attempts to resolve the Communist and Nationalist differences in China—all of which led to the eventual Communist dominance and the subsequent break in U.S. relations—there was no greater mistake than U.S. support for British ships retaking Chinese ports, fundamentally undermining China's territorial sovereignty. One might say, it was the mistake from which all other mistakes were made.

What could have been a reconciliation between the Nationalists and Communists—and then joint efforts for China's development (which would have, in all likelihood, been brokered by Franklin Roosevelt and his followers), instead, under the British and Wall Street policies of Churchill, Truman, and the Dulles brothers, resulted in our repeated failures in much of Asia over the last seventy years.[4] When combined with the complete loss of political and economic collaboration with our two greatest wartime allies, Russia and China—as measured both in total sacrifices made and length of sustained effort, as well as being the largest nations of Eurasia—there was then no option for global development, or a new Renaissance, that is, until this failure is resolved.

To give a flavor of FDR's own thinking on the subject, here is a lengthy quote from Elliott's book, *As He Saw It*, which captures the clear and distinct intentions of President Roosevelt towards the post-war world, as said directly to then-Prime Minister Winston Churchill at the Atlantic Conference, held in August, 1941 in Newfoundland, their first wartime summit. It is important to mention, that here, at the very first of their wartime summits, the Atlantic Charter, the document which later became the basis for the United Nations, was also signed.[5]

Elliott Roosevelt, from *As He Saw It*:

It must be remembered that at this time Churchill was the war leader, Father only the president of a state which had indicated its sympathies in a tangible fashion. Thus, Churchill still arrogated the conversational lead, still dominated the after-dinner hours. But the difference was beginning to be felt.

And it was evidenced first, sharply, over Empire.

Father started it.

"Of course," he remarked, with a sly sort of assurance, "of course, after the war, one of the preconditions of any lasting peace will have to be the greatest possible freedom of trade."

He paused. The P.M.'s head was lowered; he was watching Father steadily, from under one eyebrow.

"No artificial barriers," Father pursued. "As few favored economic agreements as possible. Opportunities for expansion. Markets open for healthy competition." His eye wandered innocently around the room.

Churchill shifted in his armchair. "The British Empire trade agreements" he began heavily, "are—"

Father broke in. "Yes. Those Empire trade agreements are a case in point. It's because of them that the people of India and Africa, of all the colonial Near East and Far East, are still as backward as they are."

Churchill's neck reddened and he crouched forward. "Mr. President, England does not propose for a moment to lose its favored position among the British Dominions. The trade that has made England great shall continue, and under conditions prescribed by England's ministers."

"You see," said Father slowly, "it is along in here somewhere that there is likely to be some disagreement between you, Winston, and me.

"I am firmly of the belief that if we are to arrive at a stable peace it must involve the development of backward countries. Backward peoples. How can this be done? It can't be done, obviously, by eighteenth-century methods. Now—"

"Who's talking eighteenth-century methods?"

"Whichever of your ministers recommends a policy which takes wealth in raw materials out of a colonial country, but which returns nothing to the people of that country in consideration. Twentieth-century methods involve bringing industry to these colonies. Twentieth-century methods include increasing the wealth of a people by increasing their standard of living, by educating them, by bringing them sanitation—by making sure that they get a return for the raw wealth of their community."

Around the room, all of us were leaning forward attentively. Hopkins was grinning. Commander Thompson, Churchill's aide, was looking glum and alarmed. The P.M. himself was beginning to look apoplectic.

"You mentioned India," he growled.

"Yes. I can't believe that we can fight a war against fascist slavery, and at the same time not work to free people all over the world from a backward colonial policy."

"What about the Philippines?"

"I'm glad you mentioned them. They get their independence, you know, in 1946. And they've gotten modern sanitation, modern education; their rate of il-

---

4. Japan, which was a wartime adversary, instead received our entire post-war assistance.

5. The eight principal points of the Charter were: 1. No territorial gains were to be sought by the United States or the United Kingdom; 2. Territorial adjustments must be in accord with the wishes of the peoples concerned; 3. All people had a right to self-determination; 4. Trade barriers were to be lowered; 5. There was to be global economic cooperation and advancement of social welfare; 6. The participants would work for a world free of want and fear; 7. The participants would work for freedom of the seas; 8. There was to be disarmament of aggressor nations, and a post-war common disarmament.

Franklin D. Roosevelt (left) with Winston Churchill in Casablanca, Morocco, in 1943.

literacy has gone steadily down. . . ."

"There can be no tampering with the Empire's economic agreements."

"They're artificial. . ."

"They're the foundation of our greatness."

"The peace," said Father firmly, "cannot include any continued despotism. The structure of the peace demands and will get equality of peoples. Equality of peoples involves the utmost freedom of competitive trade. Will anyone suggest that Germany's attempt to dominate trade in central Europe was not a major contributing factor to war?"

It was an argument that could have no resolution between these two men. . . .

The conversation resumed the following evening:

Gradually, very gradually, and very quietly, the mantle of leadership was slipping from British shoulders to American. We saw it when, late in the evening, there came one flash of the argument that had held us hushed the night before. In a sense, it was to be the valedictory of Churchill's outspoken Toryism, as far as Father was concerned. Churchill had got up to walk about the room. Talking, gesticulating, at length he paused in front of Father, was silent for a moment, looking at him, and then brandished a stubby forefinger under Father's nose.

"Mr. President," he cried, "I believe you are trying to do away with the British Empire. Every idea you entertain about the structure of the postwar world demon-

strates it. But in spite of that"—and his forefinger waved—"in spite of that, we know that you constitute our only hope. And"—his voice sank dramatically—"you know that we know it. You know that we know that without America, the Empire won't stand."

Churchill admitted, in that moment, that he knew the peace could only be won according to precepts which the United States of America would lay down. And in saying what he did, he was acknowledging that British colonial policy would be a dead duck, and British attempts to dominate world trade would be a dead duck, and British ambitions to play off the U.S.S.R. against the U.S.A. would be a dead duck.

Or would have been, if Father had lived.[6]

The Summit's Peak

With the kind of political transformations now occurring globally, every citizen of every nation, and of the United States most emphatically, should insist that his or her leadership, as with President Trump, is in attendance at Beijing in May. For the world needs a new economic system premised on long-term physical development, as well as the collaborations of the world's great nations, not the least between Russia, China, and the United States.

But with even greater emphasis, we must intend to launch, not just a new system, but to qualitatively transform the notion of human identity, and to set forth a new Renaissance for mankind as our great task. For a Renaissance is not one category out of many—rather it is the flourishing of a new and profound conception of human creative powers through every scientific field, every cultural expression, and through every great endeavor our society shall take.

The Beijing Summit represents a unique opportunity, not only to assemble heads of state from nations around the world to discuss global development—which itself has great relevance—but the greatest priority, the one which will shape the next 500 years and more to come, is to launch the worldwide Renaissance that Lyndon LaRouche, his wife Helga, and their associates have initiated since the 1960's.

Lyndon LaRouche Launches a Renaissance

By 1952, already facing the demise of the legacy of FDR, Lyndon LaRouche consolidated his own revolu-

---

6. *As He Saw It,* by Elliott Roosevelt (New York: Duell, Sloan and Pearce, 1946).

tionary discovery regarding human identity, a discovery which addresses the very systemic and intrinsic flaw of the British/Wall Street-dominated post-war system. In this discovery, he uniquely demonstrates that not only is the human individual and human society scientifically and demonstrably distinct from, and superior to, any animal species—but also, that the human mind cannot be replicated by, and is fundamentally superior to, any computer or digital processing system.

It was from this unique discovery that a platform was established for an entirely new aspect of long-term economic planning, and this became the basis not only for a revival of FDR's post-war worldview, but for China's "One Belt One Road" initiative, and the potential Renaissance today.

Most important, through a series of political interventions beginning in the 1960's and extending to Ronald Reagan's SDI program, LaRouche and his associates defined a qualitative leap in economic strategic science. By focusing on a commitment towards shared responsibility for exploration and development of space, largely based on advanced breakthroughs in subatomic science—e.g. fusion propulsion systems, as well as commercial fusion energy and matter/anti-matter technology—LaRouche and his associates defined the distinct challenges to be overcome for a successful new system, i.e. they had defined the commitments any nation, or groups of nations, should undertake to launch a new Renaissance for mankind.

With the advent of the Trump Presidency, after sixteen years of satanic ruin under the Bush and Obama terms, we now see a renewed potential to once again act upon the Renaissance potential that Lyndon LaRouche and his associates have created. It is increasingly likely, perhaps even in his first address to Congress, that Trump will call for a return to manned spaceflight to the Moon "before this decade is out." Such an initiative would not only spark the quality of leadership in advanced scientific fields of exploration, but would, as with a song of great beauty, strike deep at the cultural pessimism and despair which has eaten away at the members of our society.

Such a revival of a space policy, a return to the Moon and beyond, is just the beginning, but it is an essential one. With the revival of manned space flight for the development of the Moon, including industrial mining for various fuel sources including oxygen and hydrogen—as well as helium-3, which is a potent fuel for fusion propulsion and energy—a new era of human evolution is finally fulfilled.

For a Renaissance is not simply a program which addresses various categories of human activity with a renewed sense of optimism. Rather, through a valid demonstration of creative insight, which is brought to the society as a whole and which regards the very nature of human creativity itself, i.e. its power to act upon the universe free from the limitations of space and time—arises a higher quality of competence, associated with an increasing power for insight into the future. Such was Brunelleschi's cupola for the Florentine Renaissance. Such is the nature of human evolution.

As Lyndon LaRouche recently said in a discussion with associates:

Real discovery—all real discovery—is not pragmatic. It's always creative. You create something, in action, which would not have happened otherwise. In other words, everything comes in by definition itself, and does not come because it's a combination of things. It becomes a servant of an idea. But the servant of the idea was not something which was composed in a formal way...

These kinds of discoveries are not discoveries which can be quantified. They can appear to be quantified, but they're not of that character... It's like creating a solar system, or a stellar system. It is not something you make by composing it, as such. It's something that you have to call upon in order to create, to stimulate, the creation of an idea which otherwise would not exist...

The necessity is to get mankind to grasp this idea, that: where do great ideas come from? What are great ideas? What do they represent? And that's the secret of science.

Conclusion

The renewed devotion to this Renaissance legacy within the United States, and the potential to work with China, as well as Russia, on the development of what we might call "The Solar Belt and Road System," appears today as if a rare comet, which is once again passing within the Earth's night-time sky. Such opportunities are rare, and should be taken up with a great urgency and passion for the future of mankind, a future which we ultimately create.

On behalf of all Americans, past, present, and future, President Trump should act now, and set the course for mankind's future. The summit in Beijing is a platform worthy of such great endeavors.

Leibniz's 'Community of Common Destiny'

by William Jones

I am not one of those people who are solely fixated on their fatherland or any particular nation, but I concern myself with the good of the entire human species, because I consider heaven my fatherland and all well-intentioned citizens as fellow citizens. And I would rather accomplish much good in Russia, than little in Germany or some other European nations ... For my inclination and desire is concerned with the common good.

— Gottfried Leibniz to Peter the Great

Gottfried Leibniz (1646-1716)

Feb. 26—The launching by China's President Xi Jinping in September 2013 of the Silk Road Economic Belt, and a month later the 21st Century Maritime Silk Road, initiated a new era in human history. The Belt and Road, as it is now called, for the first time in decades calls for the development of the former colonial world and the elimination of poverty. And this is not simply a commitment in words, but is backed up by a major, multi-billion dollar infrastructure program that will take us through the next 30 years. The fact that China, as the country which has succeeded in bringing more people out of poverty than any country in the world, was the initiator of the project, has engendered great enthusiasm among other countries to cooperate in this endeavor.

But what lies behind the initiative is more than a simple development program. It is rather an attempt to pull the world away from the insanity of geopolitical conflicts toward a world order in which countries work together for the common good, creating a "community of common destiny," as President Xi has sometimes said. A look back at earlier attempts to create such a world by the great scientist and thinker Gottfried Leibniz—in the chaotic world of the 17th century—can perhaps give us a better understanding of the nature of the proposal being mooted today, as well as an understanding of the pitfalls this attempt is facing.

Out of the Rubble of War

The words of Gottfried Leibniz, quoted above, indicate the outlook of a man who was unusual for his time, indeed it is an outlook that is quite unusual for our time as well, and has been represented by only a handful of political leaders in this century, of which the economist and statesman Lyndon LaRouche is one. Leibniz was at the same time a patriot of his nation and a citizen of the world, as his countryman Friedrich Schiller would express it later in the century.

In his attempt to resolve the religious rancor that still gripped Europe in the aftermath of bloody religious war, Leibniz' gaze looked far beyond his country's borders in seeking a solution. And in doing so, his life and work had repercussions throughout the world, in Russia, in Asia, and indeed in North America. Our own Benjamin Franklin, active as a scientist and diplomat for the young American Republic in Eighteenth Century Paris—where the thought of Leibniz was still very much debated and discussed among Franklin's friends—could not help but be influenced by it. In seeking a new paradigm to replace the paradigm of conflict, war, and oppression that had gripped Europe for three decades, Leibniz had to embrace the entire world.

Leibniz was born in 1646. The Peace of Westphalia, signed two years later, concluded the bloody conflict of the Thirty Years' War. There were an estimated eight million casualties in that war, which had left total devastation in the heart of Europe. Famine and disease had significantly decreased the populations of Germany, Bohemia, the Low Countries, and Italy, and most of the governments were bankrupted. Entire regions were left barren, denuded by the movement of the armies.

It was in the environment of the recovery following this tremendous devastation that the young Leibniz grew up. While the Peace of Westphalia of 1648 succeeded in stopping the conflict by putting the notion of "the good of the other" at the center of the diplomatic resolution, Leibniz always sought to find a more permanent and higher-order resolution in a unity of the different religions—and nations—around a concept of the common good. While raised a Protestant—and always remaining Protestant—he initiated and engaged in a wide-ranging dialogue with representatives of many nations and different religions in striving to attain this unity.

While trained as a lawyer, his great interest was in philosophy and mathematics, indeed, Leibniz was the epitome of the great polymath, whose true slogan could have been *nihil humanum mihi alienum est*—nothing human is alien to me. His contributions in science, mathematics, geology, economics, and astronomy were a crucial element in the rapid developments in science during the Seventeenth Century. During the course of his illustrious career, Leibniz came into contact with most of the leading lights of his day, of which he soon would become one of the brightest. But his fundamental concern was for the good of humanity, and with the

Map of Eurasia, c. 1730, by J.C. Homann. China in light blue. Europe, from the North Sea to the Urals, shown as a single entity.

need to improve the lot of mankind through the continuous development and proliferation of scientific knowledge and technological innovation, and to this goal he devoted his utmost efforts.

Leibniz ended up in the employ of the Duke of Brunswick-Lüneburg, one of the smaller kingdoms in the northwest of Germany, a service which often imposed on him rather mundane tasks, far below his tremendous capabilities and his interests. While he worked to introduce technological innovations on the Duke's estates, his real work was often conducted at night, in the massive correspondence he conducted with scientists, scholars, and political figures around the world. One of these more mundane tasks was writing a history of the house of Brunswick-Lüneburg (a task which he never fully completed). But it gave him the opportunity to travel to European capitals, ostensibly to do archival research in pursuit of that history.

While many of his aristocratic employers had little concern for his broad intellectual pursuits, there were two major figures who were both supporters of his work and his confidantes, Electress Sophie of Brunswick, the wife of his employer, the Elector of Brunswick, and her daughter, Sophie Charlotte, later to become the Queen of Prussia. During a stay of several years in Paris in the service of Johann Christian von Boineberg, a privy councillor of the state of Hesse, Leibniz also established close contacts with the leading scientific figures in Jean-Baptiste Colbert's newly formed Royal Academy of Sciences in Paris, of which he would ultimately become a member. Among these was Christiaan Huygens, his senior by twenty years, who became a mentor and collaborator of the young Leibniz.

The discovery of the New World by Christopher Columbus had raised a series of interesting questions that were still unresolved in Leibniz' time. Was this new continent connected in any way with the Eurasian heartland? While Vasco Nuñez de Balboa had already discovered the Pacific Ocean, marking off North America as a continent, it was not clear if that ocean separated the two continents entirely. Most of North Asia still remained unexplored territory. This was a question that piqued young Leibniz' curiosity.

Peter the Great, by Godfrey Kneller, 1698.

The Crucial Role of Russia

With the accession of young Peter I to the Russian throne in 1682, Leibniz became aware of the new Czar's intention to bring feudal Russia into the modern era by introducing the scientific and technological advances developed in western Europe. Learning of these "heroic intentions" of the young Czar, Leibniz began looking for an opportunity to consult with Russia's new master.

His interest in Russia was also stimulated by the manifold languages found in the vast expanse of the Russian Empire, including parts of the ancient Scythian region. Even in the midst of intense discussions about politics and diplomacy, Leibniz would always ask for more light to be shed on linguistic and philological matters. He was always searching for the origins of the peoples of central Europe, most of whom had come out of Central Asia and the ancient land of Scythia. He thought that a thorough knowledge of the languages of these early settlers in the region would give him a better understanding of the ethnography of the nations of Europe.

Finally, it was Leibniz' budding interest in China that helped feed his interest in the new Russian Czar. He considered Russia as the bridge between China and the East.

There was also an important political aspect to this project. The sea route to the East was increasingly dominated by the Dutch and English. The Dutch trading power had grown and had begun to replace Portuguese dominance in the Far Eastern trade. The Dutch were also preventing the Jesuit missionaries—sent first by Portugal to the Chinese empire, to seek conversion of the people to Christianity—from landing at Goa (India) and Macau, near Hong Kong. The other nations of Europe, apart from the English, would be effectively shut out of this important trade unless a land route could be found. And the most direct land route from Europe would be through Siberia. But the new Czar showed great reluctance to open up such a route, desirous of maintaining full control of Russia's trade with the East. Leibniz thought that he could overcome that resistance.

Russia was also of great importance for Leibniz in his attempt to overcome the religious disputes which still lingered on in Europe, in spite of Westphalia. The weakness of the German states and the expansive nature of Catholic France under Louis XIV—particularly the French attempts to place a Bourbon on the Spanish throne—were roiling the uneasy post-Westphalia equilibrium between the religions. In 1685, Louis had revoked the Edict of Nantes that had allowed the French Protestant Huguenots to live and work in France, forcing them to leave their country.

Leibniz believed that a growing role for Orthodox Russia in Europe, particularly if it were built on a close collaboration with the German Protestant states, would help maintain a certain political equilibrium that might prevent a future conflict from developing across the Catholic-Protestant divide. And if such a conflict did occur, an alliance with Russia could provide an important military mainstay for the disparate forces in Germany.

There were also considerable scientific benefits, which would flow from the scientific and economic development of the Russian empire, particularly the development of Russia's Far East. Establishing the contours of the northern and eastern regions of Russia and determining whether or not there was a land connection to North America would be an important scientific advance. It was also important to begin cataloging the mineral resources of the region for future exploitation. Important experiments could be conducted in the Arctic with regard to the Earth's magnetic field and changes in it over time, to achieve a more exact calculation of longitude, which would be of tremendous benefit for navigation and shipping.

Leibniz' early exposure to China came primarily through the works he had come across in his library research and from his growing correspondence with Jesuit missionaries and others who had traveled to China. But even at the age of 22, he had felt that China possessed greater knowledge in medicine than what was available in the West. He also felt that the Chinese were much more advanced in philosophy. To establish an intellectual and philosophical connection— "commerce of light" between East and West, as Leibniz dubbed it—the role of Russia was crucial.

France Launches China Science Mission

While the Jesuits were a Catholic teaching and missionary order, they put a great deal of emphasis on developing the study of the natural sciences. In contrast to much of the Tridentine church reforms, which often stressed the tenets of faith more than, or even contrary to, the works of reason, the Jesuits effectively com-

Ferdinand Verbiest, appointed director of the Bureau of Astronomy by Emperor Kangxi.

bined the two, treating the study of nature as "reading the book" which the Creator had written. In their missionary work in China, which began in 1579, this orientation proved to be invaluable, since the advances of science in the West from the time of the great Renaissance were largely unknown in the East, and there was a growing interest in these advances among Chinese intellectuals as they began to sample some of them through the mediation of the Jesuit missionaries in the Sixteenth Century.

The Jesuit mission in China had been largely under the auspices of Portugal from the beginning. From the outset, the Jesuits aimed to convert some of the leading intellectual and political circles in China, estimating that if they could convert the leading figures, the people would soon follow. So their emphasis was always on sharpening the scholarly aspect of their work in order to gain and maintain a foothold in China. Their work required them to learn the Chinese language with sufficient fluency to read the Chinese classics, a necessary prerequisite for understanding the outlook and thinking of the Chinese intellectual elites and thus for earning their respect.

Under the Italian Jesuit, Matteo Ricci, the mission successfully adapted to the customs of the Chinese elites, putting aside their cassocks and donning the garb characteristic of Chinese intellectuals. And they were armed with the most advanced technologies coming out of the great Renaissance, with the goal of introducing the benefits of modern science to the Chinese court.

Beginning in the early Seventeenth Century, Jesuits were assigned to lead the work of the Chinese Bureau of Astronomy. Father Ferdinand Verbiest, a Belgian Jesuit and an excellent astronomer, had become a tutor of the young Emperor, Kangxi (reigned 1661-1722), and had been appointed the head of the Bureau. Seeing the need for a stronger scientific component of the mission in order to maintain the Jesuits' favorable status in the country, Verbiest sent Father Philippe Couplet to Europe in 1678 to recruit more Jesuit scientists. This initiative met with a positive response from the French King, who was eager to establish contacts in India and

China to promote French participation in the Far Eastern trade and to break the monopoly of the Dutch and Portuguese.

In 1684, François-Michel le Tellier, the Marquis de Louvois, successor to Colbert as the head of the Royal Academy of Sciences, asked the leader of the Jesuits in France for six learned men. They met at the Academy with astronomer Giovanni Domenico Cassini, the director of the Observatory of Paris, and Philippe de la Hire, a French mathematician and correspondent of Leibniz.

Cassini was intensely interested in Chinese astronomy. At this time there was much concern regarding the accuracy of the prevalent Biblical view of the age of the Earth and what therefore seemed to be exaggerated claims of the long span of Chinese culture. One way to determine the issue would be to compare the results of ancient Chinese astronomy, which had been the most advanced in its time, with that of Western astronomy. Comparing the observations of the ancient astronomers with those of the present could help determine the period of time that had lapsed in between. Leibniz was also keen on resolving this basic question.

In the course of these discussions, it was decided that the Academy would provide the assembled group of Jesuits with the necessary equipment and materials for astronomical observations. They were also instructed what observations they were to make from their Beijing Observatory as well as during their voyage to the East, with particular regard to observing the eclipses of the satellites of Jupiter, a key method of establishing longitude that had been proposed by Galileo, in which the movement of the moons of Jupiter served as a clock. The group was also assigned to investigate the flora and fauna of China and to learn other technical arts there. The Royal Academy would arrange the publication of their results in Europe and would serve as a platform for collaboration with European scientists.

The French group—dubbed "the King's Mathematicians" to avoid any conflict with the Portuguese—left Brest on March 3, 1685 under the leadership of Father

Giovanni Cassini of the Paris Observatory provided guidance to the astronomer team.

Jean de Fontaney.

Although Leibniz already had many Jesuit correspondents, including the proto-sinologist and literatus Athanasius Kircher, it was the departure of the King's Mathematicians that first fired his great enthusiasm for this endeavor in the East.

Leibniz in Rome

In 1689 Leibniz traveled to Italy. He had found a connection between the house of his patron, Brunswick-Lüneburg, and the Italian Este family, both branches of the Guelf family, and used this as a pretext to visit Italian archives. Spending several months there, he established connections with all of the major academies—in Rome, Naples, Florence, Bologna, Padua, and Venice. He also visited Mount Vesuvius, which allowed him to finish his work on volcanism, geology, and natural history, *Protogaea*. It was also on his Italian tour that Leibniz began his groundbreaking *Essay on Dynamics*, which he would publish in 1695.

In Rome, Leibniz met several times with Father Claudio Filippo Grimaldi, one of the Jesuit missionaries serving in China. Grimaldi was the vice director of the Imperial Bureau of Astronomy headed by Father Verbiest, who worked directly under the Manchu Emperor Kangxi. Grimaldi had returned from China temporarily. From Grimaldi, Leibniz received a firsthand picture of the situation in China, the work of the Jesuits in promoting science and astronomy at the Imperial court, and a sense of the Emperor's character.

Having an incredible interest in things mechanical, Kangxi had granted permission for the Jesuits to remain in China and to propagate their faith. Kangxi, embodying the character of the benevolent Confucian ruler, was devoted to creating an effective state organization that would benefit his people. From Kangxi's own writings, one detects a man devoted to the service of the nation and unwilling to accept anything less from those who served under him.

Leibniz was fascinated by Grimaldi's description of the Chinese emperor and thought that he might be of much service to Kangxi in his striving to advance the

cc/Kallgan

Equatorial armillary sphere, built before Verbiest's time, at the Beijing Ancient Observatory, founded 1442. Verbiest contributed several instruments of his own construction, including an ecliptic armillary sphere.

well-being of his nation through the introduction of modern science. Grimaldi also told Leibniz about the workings of the proto-academy the Jesuits had set up at the court, often attended by the Emperor himself. Grimaldi and Leibniz also discussed scientific issues related to the astronomical observations of the Jesuits and the nature of the work done by Chinese astronomers through the centuries.

Grimaldi would leave Rome before Leibniz, to return to Beijing. Verbiest had died while Grimaldi was away, falling from a horse on one of his missions for the Emperor, and Kangxi appointed Grimaldi to replace him.

During Leibniz' stay in Italy, Pope Innocent XI died, and Leibniz delayed his departure from Rome to see the results of the conclave to elect his successor. In the process, he had time to meet with some of the assembled cardinals. While the Protestant Leibniz was viewed by some of the conservative Church leaders with some mistrust, his reputation in the "republic of letters" gave him a particular status and opened doors at the highest level among those who were devoted to the arts and sciences. Many of the prelates, including several cardinals, were happy to meet with him.

Leibniz was also keen on helping those in the Vatican who were working to get the Church ban on Copernicus' heliocentric theory lifted. While in Rome Leibniz also met with Amable de Toureil, one of the leading

Jansenists, a Catholic movement that was accused of Calvinist leanings. De Toureil, under threat from the Inquisition, was living in Rome under the pseudonym Alberti. Because of the status of "Alberti," the two would only meet after dark in a café near the Piazza Navona.

While in Rome, Leibniz formulated a series of questions about China for which he hoped Grimaldi could obtain answers. How do the Chinese make silk? How do they fire their porcelain? What type of earth do they use as the material? What technique do they use to achieve the smooth texture and the colors? What medicines do they use? Do they know anything about modern geometry and metaphysics? Are they aware of the Pythagorean theorem? Do they know anything about the ends of the continent, especially in the Arctic region? What kind of windmills do they use? How do they transport large stones? What type of technology do they use in their mining? How do they make their sails? What are their agricultural techniques? Is there anything in their technology that would make life more comfortable here in Europe?

He also had many questions about the Chinese language and script, questions that would remain much of a mystery during Leibniz' lifetime.

Leibniz was anxious to know whether Grimaldi knew of the letter Johannes Kepler had written to Father Terrentius, another Jesuit who had been active in the Chinese mission earlier, and who had sent Kepler a report on Chinese astronomy and their celestial observations. Kepler corrected some of the calendrical inaccuracies of the Chinese astronomers and sent Terrentius his recently published Rudolphine Tables—allowing the calculation of planetary positions for any time in the past or future—to assist them in their observations.

The 'Propagation of Light and Wisdom'

Leibniz maintained a steady correspondence with Grimaldi and his fellow Jesuits for the next 15 years in an attempt to achieve that "commerce of light" which he felt would result from this East-West collaboration. In his initial letters to Grimaldi, he not only expressed a strong wish that the Fathers do their best to communicate the scientific knowledge of the West to the Chinese, but also urged them to expend every effort to transmit the wisdom of the East to the West, fearful that when the Emperor had everything he wanted from his Jesuit interlocutors, they might be asked to leave. This was a matter to which he would continually return, with a clear foreboding that this opening to the East could quickly be closed—a foreboding which was not without some basis.

The Jesuits began teaching mathematics to Kangxi in 1689. They provided their own translation of French Jesuit Ignace-Gaston Pardies' *Elémens de Géométrie* as a textbook and composed treatises in Manchu on Western arithmetic and the geometry of Euclid. "In the early 1690s, I often worked several hours a day with them," Kangxi later wrote,

> With Verbiest I had examined each stage of the forging of cannons, and made him build a water fountain that operated in conjunction with an organ, and erect a windmill in the court; with the new group—who were later joined by Brocard and Jartoux, and worked in the Yanghsin Palace under the general direction of my Eldest Son Yin-t'i—I worked on clocks and mechanics.

Kangxi was excited by the various clocks and models the Jesuits had brought with them, including a calculating machine invented by Blaise Pascal. Many of these objects can now be seen in the Palace Museum in Beijing.

Leibniz let his Jesuit interlocutors know that he had also developed a calculating machine which, like Pascal's, could add and subtract, but which could also multiply. He offered the machine to them for the benefit of the Emperor, but it was never sent. He felt that if the Emperor were excited by his device, he himself might be asked to come and advise the Emperor. But such an invitation never came. Leibniz was, nevertheless, quite taken by the descriptions of the Manchu Emperor. Leibniz would later write,

> The monarch … who almost exceeds human heights of greatness, being a god-like mortal, ruling all by a nod of his head, who, however, is educated to virtue and wisdom … thereby earning the right to rule.

In his correspondence, Leibniz informed Grimaldi of the latest developments in European science, including his own work on developing a binary system and the differential calculus, and his work on the catenary which, he explained, was essentially a logarithmic curve, and not—like Galileo had thought—a parabolic curve. He also reported on his notion of dynamics, which he had developed as a new concept in physical science. He described some of the latest developments in astronomy, reporting on Huygens' last work, *Cosmotheoros*, and on recent developments in optics, and on work on a submarine. He also provided incisive comments on the political situation in Germany.

Leibniz took responsibility for bringing knowledge of the work in China and of Chinese culture to the attention of the European public. In 1697 Leibniz, who rarely published his own works, took on the responsibility of publishing in Latin a compilation of material from the China missions, *Novissima Sinica* (Latest News from China), for which he wrote an extensive preface.

It contained contributions from Father José Suarez on the work and trials of the Jesuits in the Chinese Empire, an extensive excerpt from Verbiest's work on astronomy, a report on the visit of a Russian delegation to China on three different occasions, a letter from Father Grimaldi to Leibniz, and a description of developments leading up to the signing of the Treaty of Nerchinsk between Russia and China in 1689, in which the Jesuits in China played a crucial role.

When republished in 1699, the book also included a profile of Emperor Kangxi and a short essay by Father Joachim Bouvet on Kangxi's life and reign. Leibniz had translated the material into Latin in order to make it available to a broader public.

The year 1697, when *Novissima Sinica* was first published, was conveniently the year that Czar Peter began his semi-incognito tour of Europe, with the goal of working in the shipyards of Amsterdam to learn how to build ships. On his way to Amsterdam, he had to travel through Germany. Leibniz was eager to bring about a meeting with the Czar, but was not successful on this occasion. But he did have some assistance from his collaborators, the two Sophies, who succeeded in waylaying the Czar at Coppenbruegge after his visit to Berlin by inviting him to dinner. No doubt they briefed Leibniz thoroughly on their impressions, as Leibniz would give a full description of the Czar to his correspondents.

He was, however, quite upset that he wasn't able to

Leibniz' Novissima Sinica *with frontispiece of Emperor Kangxi (Cam-Hy).*

meet with him personally. Writing to the numismatist Andreas Morell, to whom he had sent a copy of *Novissima Sinica*, Leibniz wrote,

> You cannot imagine how upset I am that proper use is not being made of the presence of the Czar of Muscovy and those good intentions which he clearly exhibits, because to win and provide direction to the spirit of such a man as the Czar or the Emperor of China, and to imbue it with an eagerness for the glory of God and the perfection of man, is worth more than a thousand victorious battles; for on the will of such people, a million others depend.

He already had begun to penetrate the Czar's circle, establishing correspondence with Peter Lefort, the son of the Czar's most trusted foreign adviser, Francis Lefort, a Swiss officer in the Russian service, and with Nikolaus Witsen, the mayor of Amsterdam who worked closely with Peter during his lengthy stay in the city.

While Leibniz had genuine zeal for the spread of Christianity in China, he always saw that mission in ecumenical terms. In addition to his support of the Jesuits, he also privately encouraged the Protestant nations—and in particular Brandenburg, where his friend and confidante Sophie Charlotte was Queen—to send missionaries to China. Here again a land-bridge through Russia would be all important. While he befriended the Jesuit missionaries, he was aware that their missionary work, if successful, might also strengthen the Catholic power in Europe, and maintaining an equibilibrium between Protestants and Catholics was all important for maintaining peace. He also encouraged the Orthodox Peter to send his own missionaries to China as well.

Learn from China!

But the real importance of the mission for him was the transmission of the works of reason in both directions. Sometimes he would express his frustration that the priests were spending too much time in proselytizing and too little time in transmitting new knowledge in their letters. Writing to Father Bouvet in December 1697, Leibniz wrote:

> I believe that our speculative mathematics has nothing corresponding to it over there; it is for certain, however, that the long practice of many centuries has taught them an infinity of beautiful mechanical inventions and other things that we don't have. For although we may possess the better principles, nevertheless, there are particular encounters there from which one can draw thousands of wonderful consequences and find thousands of inventions. I myself am surprised all the time to see how much we lack, and how much could be added to our practice in the most useful things in life, or the most necessary, in regard to numbers, figures, machines, navigation, military science, geography, etc.

The Jesuits in China did not, however, have an easy task in China generally. The periods in which they were held in high regard, such as the period under Emperor Kangxi described here, would often be followed by times of intense persecution, depending on the intermittent strength of the opposition to the propagation of Christianity in the Chinese Empire by some Chinese intellectual layers.

But there was also growing opposition within the Catholic Church to the way the Jesuits had adopted

Confucius as a legitimate figure in the pantheon of reputable philosophers such as Plato, whose ideas, albeit not Christian, were deemed compatible with Christianity. The practice of the Jesuits in adapting to certain rites associated with Confucianism—for instance, ritually honoring one's ancestors—was deemed by some conservative Catholic elements, even those within the Jesuit order, as incompatible with Christianity. This simmering opposition, coming particularly from the Spanish Franciscan and Dominican missionaries in the Far East, would soon have devastating consequences for the survival of the Jesuit mission.

As early as the beginning of the Eighteenth Century, Leibniz was aware of the problem of this "Rites Controversy." Indeed, his publication of the *Novissima Sinica*, particularly his introduction, was his own defense of the Jesuit policy. But he was concerned that the Jesuit priests were not doing enough to investigate and transmit as much as possible of the knowledge available from China that would benefit European society, and he asked them to move quickly on this task, even at the cost of their proselytizing.

Writing in May 1703 to Joachim Bouvet, who had again mooted the possibility of a change of attitude by the Emperor toward the Jesuits, Leibniz wrote:

> Therefore it is extremely important to work on the history of the Arts of China without delay, insofar as you are able; this is more so the case, as they can learn from us more easily than we can from them, and that our teachings consist more of rationalizing, while theirs is based more on experience; and ours are readily available while theirs are little known except by those in the profession, and it is traditionally transmitted among these layers.

Leibniz even proposed that a portion of the missionaries be assigned solely to this cultural exchange while others deal with the proselytizing.

Leibniz also encouraged the establishment of an Academy in Beijing similar to what he had developed in Berlin and what he would propose and succeed in establishing in Russia. He wrote to Bouvet in July 1704:

> Is there not a basis in China, as with us, for academies, universities, and colleges of doctrine, and could not the Emperor be persuaded to set up

one for the cultivation of sciences? This task could be accomplished through his uncle, Prince Sosan, and others who are interested, and who favor you. One could open it to Tartars, Chinese, and Europeans.

In 1713, Emperor Kangxi would in fact establish such an academy, the Academy of Mathematics.

Later, in August 1705, Leibniz was even more anxious in a letter to Father Antoine Verjus:

> I fear that one day when the Chinese have learned our sciences, they will expel the Europeans. Consequently, I believe, that one should not lose the opportunity to make up for it by conducting an exchange of their knowledge for ours. For, although I see the majority of missionaries sometimes inclined to speak with contempt about the knowledge that the Chinese possess, nevertheless, their language and character, their way of life, their crafts and manufactures, even their games, are almost entirely different from ours, as if they were a people from a different globe; it is impossible that an unadorned but precise description of that which is practiced by them, would not give us considerable enlightenment, and in my view, would be more useful than all the customs and all the artifacts of the Greeks and Romans, so greatly appreciated by so many scholars.

Councillor to the Czar

But the key to really tapping this source, in Leibniz' view, lay with Russia. And Leibniz had been making some progress on that front. In a letter apparently to Peter Lefort in 1697, Leibniz had already laid out an ambitious program for Peter to map the great expanses under his rule.

In an October 1707 letter to his friend Baron Heinrich von Huyssen, who had become the tutor to the children of the Czar, Leibniz wrote:

> As China is an almost entirely different world from ours in an infinity of things, my curiosity has turned totally in that direction; and I believe the Czar's Empire can establish a liaison between China and Europe, since it in fact touches on both. I will soon be coming to speak with a missionary who came from there. He is a bit

anti-Jesuit, but that doesn't keep him for working with them on matters of making known all that they have learned there.

In November 1711, Leibniz wrote to James Bruce, a Scottish general in the service of the Czar:

I hear that His Majesty the Czar has had people travel from Siberia to the Arctic and the ice cape, and I would like to know what they have brought back with them and whether they have been able to determine if there is a land connection between Asia and America, which many believe there is, but others deny. No one can better resolve that question than the Czar, and its resolution would bring him much greater fame than the Egyptian Pharoah who discovered the source of the Nile. The Chinese monarch is also conducting geographic and astronomical observations, about which I have received correspondence. I hope that the Chancellery will not forget my humble services.

Leibniz was also instrumental in helping to arrange the marriage of the Czar's son, Czarevich Alexei, to Charlotte, the daughter of the Duke of Wolfenbüttel, creating closer ties to a court with which Leibniz was on very close terms. It was through the Duke that Leibniz was finally able to get an audience with the Czar in Torgau in 1711, when the Czar came to Germany to arrange his son's marriage.

There Leibniz presented him with a broad program of development for Russia, which included plans for establishing a printing trade and publishing facilities, building secondary schools, improving agriculture, conducting research on variations in the magnetic declination of the Earth in Russia, gathering knowledge of slavonic languages, promoting manufacturing and, most important of all, founding an academy of sciences, similar to the one he had helped create, and was leading, in Berlin.

In this audience Leibniz also raised the possibility of mapping Siberia, improving the sea- and land-routes to China and the East, and Leibniz's own plan for sending an expedition to find a possible land connection between Asia and North America.

Leibniz also spoke of the need for Russia to establish closer relations with the Chinese Emperor and promised to send some of the correspondence he had had with China to the Czar for his own enlightenment on this matter.

In a letter to the Czar, Leibniz explained his intentions:

It seems to be the hand of God that science begins to encompass the entire world and should now come to the Scythians, and that Your Majesty serves as the tool to accomplish this as you can take the best from Europe and the best from China and what both have provided you can improve on through good institutions.

In a second meeting with the Czar the following year, Leibniz was officially made a councillor to the Czar, but, to his chagrin, received no invitation to travel to Russia in that capacity. He did, however, serve as an envoy of the Czar in arranging a treaty between the Holy Roman Emperor, with whom Leibniz was on good terms, and the Russian Empire, as Peter was still in a major conflict with Sweden and sought allies in Europe.

In this new position, Leibniz continued to put proposals to the Czar for the development of science in Russia. And while his desire for Peter to allow free travel through the Russian Empire to China for missionaries and others would not be realized in his lifetime, many of his proposals would be implemented and would lay the basis for the development of science in Russia during the following century. As the great Russian scientist Vladimir Vernadsky once noted in his history of this era, the first Russian scientist was Peter himself. And behind Peter stood the great German thinker and scientist, Gottfried Leibniz.

Arrogance Closes the Door to China

As Leibniz had feared, the end would come for the Jesuit mission in China, but not because of some arbitrary decision by Kangxi, but rather by the obtuseness and arrogant behavior of conservative circles in the Vatican. At issue was the role of Confucius and the status of Confucian rites. Conservative opponents in the Vatican said that Confucius and the cult of Confucius was a religion, and a heathen one at that, and was therefore in contradiction with the teachings of the Church. The Jesuits and their defenders, including Leibniz, said that the rites connected with Confucius were a civil ceremony and not a religious service. Kangxi himself asserted publicly that this was the case.

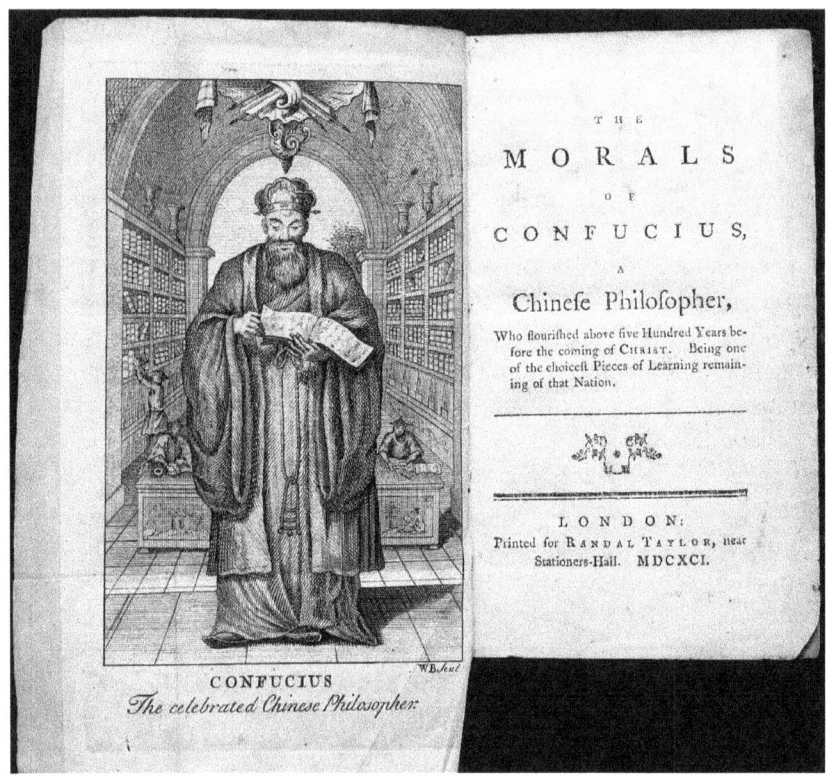

Confucius, in a 1691 English rendition of a selection from his Analects, as translated by Fathers Philippe Couplet and Prospero Intorcetta.

But this was not enough for the traditionalists in the Vatican. They persuaded Pope Clement XI to rule against the Jesuits in 1704, issuing a decree, *Cum Deus optimus*, to the effect that Chinese Catholics would not be allowed to participate in any of the ceremonies, or visit any of the temples, associated with Confucius, except Christian officials in their offical capacity.

The Emperor was furious, but held out the hope that this decision could be reversed. The Pope then sent Monsignor Charles-Thomas Tournon to China to carry out his orders. Tournon, an arrogant and irascible diplomat, angered the Emperor, who banished him to Macao in 1707 and threw his assistant in jail. The Pope rewarded Tournon with a cardinal's hat, but he died soon afterward in Macao.

But even then Kangxi did not issue a ban, but rather a ruling saying that all the missionaries who wished to stay and follow the practice of Ricci on the question of the Rites, would be allowed to do so if they were willing to remain in China for life. Then in 1715, Clement issued a Bull *Ex illa die* (From that day), which reiterated his condemnation of the Confucian Rites. He went even further in this Bull, saying that even Catholic of-

ficials in China could not even participate in their formal status in such rites. Kangxi commented, "I have never heard such utter nonsense." In retaliation, Kangxi issued that year a Red Edict, which expelled all missionaries except Father Bouvet, who was allowed to remain in his role as a scientist. A year later Kangxi issued a ban against the spread of Christianity in China.

The door to China had been closed again by the obstinacy of those in the West who did not understand the advantage of this cooperation. But the achievements remained. As Han Qi of the Chinese Academy of Sciences reports in a paper written on Sino-French scientific relations in the Seventeenth Century:

The measurements taken in China of lunar and solar eclipses, of Jupiter's satellites, comets, and the passage of Mercury through the solar disk were all used to determine longitudes and latitudes in China and to calculate the route of the comet that appeared in Beijing in 1699 and 1742. Observing magnetic declination was very helpful to correct Halley's tables, which were often used by scientists. The results of the work of the Jesuit astronomers helped determine the shape of the Earth and the obliquity of the ecliptic.[1]

And the knowledge of China transmitted to the West through this work was instrumental in broadening the understanding of the work of Confucius and of Chinese philosophy among the world's scientists and scholars, including our Benjamin Franklin.

Now we have another such opportunity with the Belt and Road Initiative. It is the responsibility of Western leaders and our own President not to lose that chance.

---

1. Han Qi. "Sino-French Scientific Relations Through the French Jesuits and the Académie Royale des Sciences in the Seventeenth and Eighteenth Centuries," in: *China and Christianity: Burdened Past, Hopeful Future*, Stephan Uhalley and Xiaoxin Wu (eds.). Studies of the Ricci Institute for Chinese-Western Cultural History. Armonk, N.Y. and London: Routledge, 2001. Pp. 137-147.

II. The New Physical Economy

Exploring the Stars With LaRouche's Four Laws

by Tony Papert

Feb. 26—Some of you reading this today will later go on to become astronauts, exploring new worlds. That is the significance of a piece of non-fake news (at last) which the *Washington Post* covered on Feb. 15. It wrote that "President Trump has indicated that he wants to make a splash in space. During his transition, he spoke with historian Douglas Brinkley about John F. Kennedy's famous 1961 vow to go to the Moon before the decade was out.

"Now Trump and his aides may do something very similar: demand that NASA send astronauts to orbit the Moon before the end of" 2019. The *Post* goes on to note that NASA had planned to test its new rocket, the Saturn-V class SLS, with the Orion astronaut capsule, in an unmanned mission in late 2018. No manned launch was planned until several years later—but now, President Trump's Administration has ordered NASA to study the possibility of adding astronauts to that first flight, for a manned orbit around the Moon before the end of 2019.

Space News reported Feb. 24 that NASA Associate Administrator Bill Gerstenmaier said the study should be ready in about a month.

NASA

President John F. Kennedy calling for the establishment of a Space Program at a Joint Session of Congress, May 25, 1961.

We need to go look at what do we really gain by putting crew on this flight. Does this really advance significantly our overall ability to get to a capability to take humans, routinely as it can be, to the vicinity of the Moon and operate safely?

Deputy Associate NASA Administrator Bill Hill added:

We know it's going to take a significant amount of money, and money that will be required fairly quickly to implement what we need to do.

In related developments, President Trump has not yet announced his choice for NASA Administrator, but *Space News* and other media claim that three persons are being considered most closely:

• Rep. Jim Bridenstine (R-OK), who is actively campaigning for the appointment,
• Former NASA Administrator Mike Griffin, and
• Highly-decorated test-pilot and astronaut Eileen Collins.

Eileen Collins addressed the Republican Convention, but reportedly did not endorse Donald Trump in her talk. We have no other knowledge of her views at this time, but we do know a lot about the other two.

Rep. Bridenstine was a Navy pilot. Part of his campaign for the NASA position was a substantial Dec. 29 blog post, "Why the Moon Matters."

Although he does not mention Lyndon LaRouche, he bases his policy for returning to the Moon as a base to conquer space, on Ronald Reagan's Strategic Defense Initiative which LaRouche designed. He goes on to urge development of lunar resources in a manner reminiscent of Krafft Ehricke, writing, for example:

From the discovery of water ice on the Moon until this day, the American objective should have been a permanent outpost of rovers and machines, with occasional manned missions for science and maintenance, in order to utilize the materials and energy of the Moon to drive down the costs and increase the capabilities of American operations in cis-lunar and interplanetary space.

This is also the first step for manned missions deeper into our solar system. A permanent human presence on other celestial bodies requires *in situ* resource utilization. The Moon, with its three-day emergency journey back to Earth, represents the best place to learn, train, and develop the necessary technologies and techniques for *in situ* resource utilization and an eventual long term human presence on Mars. Fortunately, the Space Launch System and Orion will start testing in 2018. This system, with a commercial lander, could quickly place machines and robots on the Moon to begin the cis-lunar economy. With the right presidential guidance, humans could return in short order as well; this time, to stay.

Former Congressman Jim Bridenstine (R-Okla.)

Bridenstine.house.gov

Bridenstine concludes:

Space utilization has transformed the human condition, including how we communicate, navigate, produce food and energy, conduct banking, predict weather, and perform disaster relief. While many of these gains are a result of private investment and commercial markets, they are only possible because the United States government took the lead and retired risk for these capabilities. Today, we are experiencing a space renaissance... A renewed focus on utilizing the Moon can help further these advances and achievements. The choices we make now can forever make America the pre-eminent spacefaring nation.

The second candidate, Mike Griffin, is well known to us. After a career as a leading aerospace engineer and executive, he was the NASA Admistrator who resigned when Obama cancelled the Constellation program, a cancellation for which Lyndon LaRouche said that Obama merited impeachment. Griffin fully agrees on a permanent return to the Moon as a base for the exploration of Mars and beyond.

Wikipedia reports:

In 2004 testimony to Congress on the future of human spaceflight, he stated, "for me the single overarching goal of human space flight is the human settlement of the Solar System, and eventually beyond. I can think of no lesser purpose sufficient to justify the difficulty of the enterprise, and no greater purpose is possible." In his testimony he also advocated heavy-lift launch capabilities, development of space-qualified nuclear power systems, *in situ* resource utilization, and cost-effective medium-size transport to low Earth orbit.

Like President Trump, Mike Griffin questions pre-

Former NASA Administrator Mike Griffith (left) resigned when Obama cancelled the Constellation program. On the right is NASA Associate Administrator Bill Gerstenmaier.

NASA/Kim Shiflett

sumed anthropogenic global warming and the measures being taken against it.

Now all of the above corresponds to the well-advertised views of President Trump himself. Although his critics of the British imperial faction continually repeat that President Trump's views and policies are some sort of "mystery," there is in fact no recent Presidential candidate other than Lyndon LaRouche, who has made his policies so crystal-clear as Donald Trump has, and repeatedly so.

Last Oct. 25, for example, Candidate Donald Trump told a rally in Sanford, Florida:

I will free NASA from the restriction of serving primarily as a logistics agency for low-Earth orbit activity—big deal. Instead, we will refocus its mission on space exploration. Under a Trump Administration, Florida and America will lead the way into the stars.

A cornerstone of my policy is we will substantially expand public-private partnerships to maximize the amount of investment and funding that is available for space exploration and development. This means launching and operating major space assets, right here, that employ thou-

sands and spur innovation and fuel economic growth.

In his Jan. 20 Inaugural Address, President Trump said:

We stand at the birth of a new millennium, ready to unlock the mysteries of space, and to free the Earth from the miseries of disease.

But for Lyndon LaRouche's tireless work over so many decades, we could never have attained the possibilities which are so evident today to everyone who is not totally morally blind. But for Lyndon LaRouche's leadership into the future, these never-before-seen opportunities, which embody the dreams and aspirations of all past generations of humanity, as Krafft Ehricke understood, would be missed and lost. The realization of these hopes requires Lyndon LaRouche's "Four New Laws" of June, 2014.

How To Win President Trump's War on Drugs

by Robert Ingraham

Feb. 24—In 1978, the LaRouche political movement published a book, *Dope. Inc.: Britain's Opium War Against the U.S.*[1] A second, expanded, version of that book was published in 1986. In his Dedication to the first edition, Lyndon LaRouche began by saying:

> *It is with proper pride that we dedicate this book to the often-unsung U.S. intelligence and law enforcement officers who have so often, so obscurely, died or languished in undeserved imprisonment in the silent war of the United States against the British monarchy's illegal drug traffic into our nation.*

It is with the same pride and the same determination that we, today, must call forth both the courage and resources necessary to finish the war which LaRouche initiated almost forty years ago.

What is required is **Total War**, in the sense of Sheridan in the Shenandoah Valley or Grant in the Overland campaign. No half-measures nor compromises with the enemy are acceptable. This is not an anti-drug "campaign"; it is war, and the only ultimate outcome must be the complete destruction of the drug cartels, i.e. Unconditional Surrender.

In a speech before the Major Cities Police Chiefs Association (MCCA) on Feb. 8, 2017, President Donald Trump stated:

Cover image from Dope, Inc.

We're going to stop the drugs from pouring in. We're going to stop those drugs from poisoning our youth, from poisoning our people. We're going to be *ruthless* in that fight. We have no choice. And we're going to take that fight to the drug cartels and work to liberate our communities from their terrible grip of violence.

Since the delivery of that speech, the President has named Department of Homeland Security Secretary Gen. John Kelly to lead the anti-drug effort, and on Feb. 9, he issued an Executive Order naming the newly confirmed Attorney General, Jeff Sessions, to be the head of a new Task Force "to focus on destroying transnational criminal organizations and drug cartels," with a 120 day mandate to report on "transnational criminal organizations and subsidiary organizations, including the extent of penetration of such organizations into the United States." That Executive Order also states:

Transnational criminal organizations and subsidiary organizations, including transnational drug cartels, have spread throughout the nation, threatening the safety of the United States and its citizens.... These groups are drivers of crime, corruption, violence, and misery.... In particular, the trafficking by cartels of controlled substances has triggered a resurgence in deadly drug abuse and a corresponding rise in violent crime related to drugs.... A comprehensive and decisive approach is required to dismantle these or-

---

1. Available at: http://store.larouchepub.com/product-p/eirbk-20-10-1-0-0-std.htm

ganized crime syndicates and cartels can be mopped up relatively easily.

These actions by the President, represent the first time, since the efforts of Ronald Reagan in 1981,[2] to seriously challenge the global power of Dope. Inc. A team is being assembled. The intention is there. The opportunity is real, and it must not be squandered. This is a war which must not be lost.

I. Casualties of War

The mass drugging of the American people is a secret hidden in plain sight. Over a span of four decades, Americans have consented to a deluge of drug usage. The responsibility for this lies at the feet of the pro-drug Wall Street establishment, the pro-drug news media, pro-drug politicians, the pro-drug psychiatric profession, and the drug-saturated Hollywood industry. An environment has been deliberately created in which everyday drug usage is seen as acceptable, if not normal or even desirable. This is the 21st Century fulfillment of the "soma" vision of British oligarch Aldous Huxley.

Current estimates are that during the last thirty day period, more than 27 million Americans used an illegal drug. During the last twelve months, at least 47 million Americans used an illegal drug. *That is 15% of the total population.*[3] Additionally, those figures do not include either the millions who legally consume a wide variety of mind-numbing prescription drugs, nor the millions of alcohol addicts.

If one were to add in the number of people who le-gally use opioids (such as OxyContin), anti-depressants (such as Prozac, Zoloft, or Celexa), anti-anxiety drugs (such as Xanax), and ADHD Drugs (such as Ritalin or Adderall), then the total figures for "drug usage" sky-rocket. The numbers are staggering.

Let us be clear: This is the deliberate mass drug enslavement of the American people. Nothing like this has existed anywhere in the world, of this scope or magnitude, since the enforced opium addiction of tens of millions of Chinese by the British monarchy in the 19th and early 20th Centuries.

Much attention is given, and rightly so, to the crime and deaths which result from illegal drug trafficking. Yet, much more devastating damage is being done. A minimum of 25%—or perhaps a much, much higher number—of the American people are now being stupe-fied by drugs. Their minds are impaired. Their cognitive reasoning is damaged. Ask yourself, would we have a society today in which tens of millions oppose nuclear power and embrace the anti-scientific fraud of global warming were it not for the widespread drugging of the population? Would we have a culture dominated by Hollywood trash and mindless video games were it not for widespread drug usage? Or, more to the point, what percentage of the deluded demonstrators who are now out on the street demanding that Donald Trump be removed from office have consumed a mind-altering drug within the last thirty days?

Reasoned discussion, which is only possible through higher cognitive functioning, a mandatory pre-requisite for the existence of a republic, is being erased from our society.

In this Case ... Figures Don't Lie

The consensus among government reports is that:

• 25 million Americans have used marijuana within the last 30 days (including 35% of high school seniors) and 41 million within the last 12 months and in addition, current figures show that, among "regular users"—i.e. those who have used the drug within the last thirty days—there are:

• 1.5 million cocaine users,
• at least 1 million heroin users (compared with 300,000 in 2003),
• 900,000 methamphetamine users,
• 3 million Ecstacy (MDMA) users,
• 2 million users of hallucinogens, and
• perhaps as many as 4 million users of illegal opioids.

---

2. President Reagan's War on Drugs was itself greatly influenced and strongly backed by Lyndon LaRouche, including the 1978 publication of *Dope, Inc.*, the founding of the National Anti-Drug Coalition, which published the first edition of its *War on Drugs* magazine in June 1980, and the personal advisory role of Lyndon LaRouche to the Reagan Administration in the early 1980s. On March 9, 1985, LaRouche delivered a speech titled "A Proposed Multi-National Strategic Operation against the Drug Traffic for the Western Hemisphere," to an anti-drug conference in Mexico City. More will be said about the content of that speech later in this report.

3. Many figures and statistics will be cited here. Every effort was made to verify their accuracy. Individual citations will not be given, but sources include the Centers for Disease Control (CDC), the *Journal of the American Medical Association* (JAMA), the U.S. Substance Abuse and Mental Health Services Administration (SAMHSA), the U.S. National Survey on Drug Use and Health, the journal *Psychotherapy and Psychosomatics*, and a variety of other government and private institutions.

If one were to expand this to include "casual users," i.e., those who have used the drug within the last year, the figures would double, or in some cases triple.

There is also the following to consider.

When *Dope, Inc.* was published in 1978, the explosion in use of legal psychiatric drugs was still two decades into the future. Today, the "legal" drugging of Americans is beyond epidemic proportions. The first anti-anxiety drug Valium was introduced in 1963, but the real revolution came with the introduction of the powerful anti-depressant Prozac in 1988, i.e., the acceptance of the idea that psychological and emotional "well-being" could be achieved through swallowing a pill. This re-definition of mind-altering drugs as "medicine"—which today includes marijuana—has been key to the mass drugging of the population.

According to figures supplied by IMS Health, a company that provides information, services and technology for the healthcare industry, **79 million** Americans are now taking some form of drug for emotional or psychological relief. *That's 25% of the entire U.S. population.* This includes

- 37 million taking anti-anxiety drugs,
- 41 million taking anti-depressants,
- 11 million taking drugs for Attention Deficit Disorder, and
- 7 million taking anti-psychotic drugs.

One in eight Americans now takes an antidepressant medication; among women in their 40s and 50s, the figure is one in four. Many people have multiple prescriptions for a variety of these drugs.

U.S. Department of Justice

Deputy Attorney General James M. Cole, on May 31, 2011.

Additionally, in 2012, 259 million prescriptions were written for narcotic opioids (e.g., Oxy-Contin), which is more than enough to give every American adult his or her own bottle of pills.

The powerful anti-anxiety and anti-panic drug Xanax today ranks #1 as the most prescribed psychiatric drug in America. As of 2015, doctors were writing nearly 50 million prescriptions for Xanax every year—*that's more than one Xanax prescription every second.*

The drugging begins at an early age. In the age group 0-5 years, 200,000 are already on ADHD drugs, 110,000 are on anti-depressants, and *725,000* are on anti-anxiety drugs. Over one million children are on drugs by the time of their sixth birthday. An astounding 20% of high school-age boys—ages 14-17—in the United States have been diagnosed with ADHD, and 10% of high school-age girls have likewise been diagnosed.

These are powerful drugs. During the last thirty years Dr. Peter Breggin has authored a series of books, including *Toxic Psychiatry*; *Talking Back to Prozac*; *Talking Back to Ritalin*; and *Medication Madness*. In his work, Dr. Breggin had documented a widespread deterioration of mental functioning in the users of these drugs. He has described a condition which he calls *Medication Spellbinding*, wherein severe mental impairment occurs without the drug user noticing it. The same could certainly be said for marijuana users.

Obama the Drug Pusher

In October 2009, Deputy Attorney General David W. Ogden issued a memorandum to federal prosecutors, directing them that they should not enforce federal anti-drug laws (the Controlled Substances Act) against individu-

DAVID OGDEN
Deputy Attorney General
C-SPAN 2
C-SPAN

David W. Ogden, Assistant Attorney General, 2009.

als or institutions which are in "clear and unambiguous compliance with existing state laws providing for the medical use of marijuana." Thus, Barack Obama became the first U.S. President to accept the definition of marijuana, a Schedule I controlled substance, as a "medicine."

This federal endorsement of marijuana was taken a step further in 2013 when Deputy Attorney General James M. Cole issued a memo to federal prosecutors in all fifty states declaring that the Obama Administration would not challenge laws legalizing marijuana in Colorado, Washington, or any other state which chose to violate federal drug laws.

In March 2015, following the legalization of marijuana in Washington, Oregon, Alaska, and Colorado, Barack Obama conducted an interview with *Vice News.* He stated that he was "encouraged" by recent actions at the state level to give greater access to marijuana. This Presidential endorsement, combined with federal non-enforcement of the nation's anti-drug laws has resulted in four additional states—California, Maine, Massachusetts, and Nevada—legalizing marijuana within the last twenty-four months.

As this article is being written, Barack Obama, together with his wife Michelle and his bizarre political bedfellow Valery Jarrett, have established a headquarters in Washington, D.C. from which to organize an effort to block and destroy President Donald Trump. This unholy trio are linked in their efforts with Nazi-sympathizer George Soros, the billionaire who is now personally bankrolling the attempt to create a "color revolution" in the United States by deploying thousands of deluded foot soldiers into the streets of American cities in violent anti-Trump demonstrations.

Since 1994, George Soros has spent more than $200 million of his own money to legalize drugs in the United States. During the last twenty years, almost every state ballot initiative for drug legalization or "decriminalization" has been financed by Soros, some

World Economic Forum/swiss-image.ch/Photo Michele Limina
George Soros at the World Economic Forum, Jan. 23, 2015.

almost entirely by him, and Soros has not limited his efforts to marijuana legalization. He has also spoken out—and financed ballot initiatives—for the decriminalization of all "hard drugs," including heroin, cocaine, and methamphetamines.

In a December 2015 interview with the Russia-24 TV channel, Viktor Ivanov, the head of the Russian anti-drug agency FSKN, charged that Soros' efforts for drug legalization in the United States, was developed for export to foreign countries, particularly intended to effect drug legalization in Mexico and other Latin American nations, where propaganda is being spread by Soros-controlled NGOs.

What Obama Has Wrought

Between 2009 and 2016, under Barack Obama:

- Marijuana use went up 100%,
- Methamphetamine use increased 62%,
- Heroin use increased 200%.

According to a report issued by the CDC, in 2012 the number of people using heroin for the first time was 156,000, nearly double the number of people in 2006. This increase has been driven largely by young adults aged 18-25.

On Feb. 23, 2017, the National Center for Health Statistics (NCHS) released data showing that overdose-related deaths increased from 38,329 in 2010 to 52,404 by 2015, a 27% increase in five years. At the same time heroin-related deaths *quadrupled*, going from 3,036 in 2010 to 12,989 in 2015 all of this under the Obama regime.

Numerous studies have documented that this frightening explosion of drug usage correlates directly to states that have legalized the Obama-approved "medical" use of marijuana. A 2014 report titled "The Effect of Medical Marijuana Laws on Marijuana, Alcohol, and Hard Drug Use," documents a 27% increase for marijuana use in states that have legalized medical marijuana.

Since the 2012 outright legalization of marijuana in Colorado and Washington, attempts have been made to calculate the effects of legalization on drug usage (as well as in the six additional states that subsequently enacted marijuana legalization). Initial studies have shown a sharp increase in drug usage among the population. Millions of youth are now being told that marijuana is a "medicine,"— like the pills that mother takes for her "well-being"—or at the very least it is acceptable to use, now that it has been legalized. The societal and cultural barriers to drug usage are being removed.

As for prescription drug use, under Obama, the overall use of psychiatric drugs to numb and pacify the population has increased dramatically. Since 2008, there has been an 87% increase in the use of anti-depressants; a 100% increase in children, under age 10, taking anti-psychotic medications, and a 40% increase in the number of girls being prescribed ADHD medications. There has been an explosion in the use of prescription opioids, accompanied by the development and marketing of new opioids, such as U-47700, which is eight times more potent than heroin. U-47700, or "pinky" as it is known, is now legal in 46 states and has been linked to many, many deaths. The United States makes up only 4.6% of the world's population, but consumes 80% of its opioids.

II. Start from the Top

So, what is to be done?

The first step must be to recognize the paramount role of the major British and American banking institutions in the global drug trade. This role is not merely one of avaricious "money laundering." The London and Wall Street apparatus is the command center for the *intended* drugging of the population, and none of the

White House Photo

President Barak Obama

major drug cartels could function without the protection and support of Wall Street and the City of London.

In 2009, Antonio Maria Costa, then the Executive Director of the United Nations Office on Drugs and Crime (UNODC), identified the fact that the international banks had become "drug dependent." He said:

In many instances, the money from drugs was the only liquid investment capital. In the second half of 2008, liquidity was the banking system's main problem and hence liquid capital became an important factor. Inter-bank loans were funded by money that originated from the drugs trade and other illegal activities... There were signs that some banks were rescued that way.

Speaking in Washington, D.C. in 2011, Viktor Ivanov, the Director of the Russian Federal Narcotics Service, went even further:

Drug money and global drug trafficking are actually not just valuable elements of, but as donors of scarce liquidity, a vital and indispensable segment of the whole monetary system.

Ivanov went on to say that Russia and the United States must work in tandem to effect the

drastic transformation of the international financial system.... To a certain extent, we are observing a revival of the logic of the Glass-Steagall Act, adopted in the U.S. in 1933 at the height of the Great Depression, which separated the deposit and investment functions of banks.

However, he added, "restrictions to prevent the attraction of criminal money are required even more. In other words, liquidation of the financial bubble alone will not be enough.... The key way to liquidate global drug trafficking is to reformat the existing economy and shift to an economy that excludes criminal money" and moves instead "to an economy of development, in which decisions are based on development projects and long-term targeted credits."

The first action which must be undertaken to combat the drug scourge is to enact into law the restoration of Franklin Roosevelt's **Glass-Steagall** legislation, along with accompanying actions which ruthlessly bring to an end the last two decades era of unregulated banking and financial speculation. The predatory practices of the "too-big-to-fail" banks in London and New York—the headquarters of Dope Inc.—have brought the trans-Atlantic financial system to ruin. The restoration of Glass-Steagall is essential for the creation of a Hamiltonian Credit System needed to finance a national economic recovery, but it will also have the salutary effect of destroying the financial operations and structures which control and bankroll the international drug trade.

The British Crown

In *Dope, Inc.*, the British monarchy's control over world-wide drug trafficking is fully documented, in an unbroken line, stretching back to the late 18th Century. As the book says, drug trafficking is the "biggest business in the world." In 1978, the authors of *Dope, Inc.* estimated that the dollar amount of world-wide drug trafficking totaled about $200 billion. Eight years later, in the 1986 edition, that estimate was raised to $500-$700 billion.

Today, global drug proceeds are in the multiple trillions of dollars. All of this money is deposited within the major financial institutions of the trans-Atlantic banking system, with a major role being played by the completely unregulated "offshore" banks, located primarily in current or former British and Dutch colonies.

This transformation of Britain into the controller of the world's largest drug cartel was signaled as early as 1776, when Adam Smith, in his *Wealth of Nations*, advocated a massive increase in opium production in India and sales into China, under the control of the East India Company. The direction and financing for this global drug empire was placed in the hands of British banks and trading companies such as Jardine-Matheson and the Hong Kong & Shanghai Bank. Many of the individuals who proved most resourceful in expanding the drug trade were knighted by Queen Victoria and her successors. The wealth of the City of London multi-plied as the dead bodies of it's victims crept into the millions.

This royal drug empire continued to operate *openly* well into the 20th Century. Between 1909 and 1914, four international conferences were held, all at American insistence, aimed at curbing the drug trade. All failed due to British opposition. In 1923, an American proposal was brought before the League of Nations to reduce worldwide opium production by 90%. It was killed by the British delegation.

During this period, the British were actually expanding their drug pushing. In 1927 official British government figures showed that in many of Britain's Asian colonies, including Malaysia, Borneo and Sarawak, profits from the drug trade accounted for over 30-50% of the government's revenues. In India, during the same period, Mahatma Gandhi was leading demonstrations against Britain's plans to *expand opium production*. Throughout this whole period, the minutes of the Advisory Committee of the League's Opium Commission document the British government's continued role in the trafficking and distribution of opium and heroin. Most people think of the Opium Wars as a 19th Century occurrence, but as late as 1937, there were 70 million opium and heroin addicts in China, all being supplied by the British government, British banks, and British trading companies..

Today, the premier British drug bank, the Hong Kong and Shanghai Bank, now known as HSBC, is still openly involved in drug financing. When it was caught red-handed in 2012 laundering billions of dollars for the Mexican and Colombian drug cartels, the Obama Administration ruled that under no circumstances would any HSBC official be criminally prosecuted for drug money laundering. On all matters related to drugs, banking, and war, Obama has always obeyed the Queen.

The words of Viktor Ivanov and Antonio Maria Costa should be taken to heart. Today, the entire bankrupt trans-Atlantic banking system is being propped up by drug money. For some, this is deliberate policy. For others they have simply become addicts who can't exist without the drug cash.

III. Total War

As in the case of William T. Sherman, as he marched through Georgia freeing slaves and burning plantations, ours must be an approach of total war. Every resource must be mobilized. During the Battle of Stalingrad, as new Soviet tanks were being produced behind the lines, those tanks rolled out of the factories and drove straight to the battlefield, many arriving within 24 to 48 hours. A commitment to such a "full mobilization" is required today.

In this regard, at this point in our report, it is best to turn to the proposals made by Lyndon LaRouche in 1985.[4] That speech is several pages long, so we will present here only brief excerpts. LaRouche begins,

> It is clear to the governments fighting the international drug-traffickers, that the drug-traffic could never be defeated if each of our nations tried to fight this evil independently of the other nations of this Hemisphere. If the drug-traffickers' laboratories are shut down in Colombia, new laboratories open up in Brazil. If the route into Florida and Georgia is attacked heavily enough, the drug-traffickers reopen routes into California, through Belize and Mexico. If Mexico shuts down drug-routes through its territory, the drug-traffickers will use Pacific routes into the U. S. states of Washington and Oregon, through the marijuana-traffickers of Hawaii....
>
> It is impossible to break the ominously increasing political power of the drug-traffickers in Mexico, Colombia, Venezuela, and other countries, without capturing the billions of dollars of drug-revenues run through corrupt banking institutions. Without help of closer cooperation between the United States, Mexico, Colombia, Venezuela, and other nations of this Hemisphere, neither the United States nor any of the other republics could defeat the monstrously powerful complex of criminal, financial, and political forces who are behind the international drug-traffic. The purpose of my remarks today, is to outline to you a proposed war-plan, for cooperative action against the international drug-traffickers, by the governments of this Hemisphere committed to that action.

LaRouche then goes on to enunciate a fifteen-point plan of action to win the War on Drugs. Here we high-light just a few of his proposals.

- The international drug traffic has become an evil and powerful government in its own right. It represents today a financial, political, and military power greater than that of entire nations within the Americas. It is a government which is making war against civilized nations, a government upon which we must declare war, a war which we must fight with the weapons of war, and a war which we must win in the same spirit the United States fought for the unconditional defeat of Nazism between 1941 and 1945...
- Law-enforcement methods must support the military side of the War on Drugs: a) Any person caught in trafficking of drugs, is to be classed as either a traitor in time of war, or as the foreign spy of an enemy power; b) Any person purchasing unlawful substances, or advocating the legalization of traffic in such substances, or advocating leniency in anti-drug military or law-enforcement policy toward the production or trafficking in drugs, is guilty of the crime of giving aid and comfort to the enemy in time of war...
- A treaty of alliance for conduct of war, should be established between the United States and the governments of Ibero-American states which join the War on Drugs alliance...
- Under the auspices of this treaty, provisions for actions of a joint military command should be elaborated. These provisions should define principles of common action, to the effect that necessary forms of joint military and law-enforcement action do not subvert the national sovereignty of any of the allied nations on whose territory military operations are conducted...
- Borders among the allied nations, and borders with other nations, must be virtually hermetically sealed against drug traffic across borders. All unlogged aircraft flying across borders or across the Caribbean waters, which fail to land according to instructions, are to be shot down by military action. A thorough search of all sea, truck, rail, and other transport, including inbound container traffic, is to be effected at all borders and other points of customs-inspection. Massive concentration with aid of military forces must be made in border-crossing areas, and along relevant arteries of internal highway and water-borne transport...
- A system of total regulation of financial institutions,

4. See: http://www.larouchepub.com/eiw/public/1985/eirv12n13-19850402/eirv12n13-19850402_036-a_proposed_strategic_operation_a-lar.pdf

to the effect of detecting deposits, outbound transfers, and inbound transfer of funds, which might be reasonably suspected of being funds secured from drug trafficking, must be established and maintained...

- All real estate, business enterprises, financial institutions, and personal funds, shown to be employed in the growing, processing, transport, or sale of unlawful drugs, should be taken into military custody immediately, and confiscated in the manner of military actions in time of war...

- The primary objective of the War on Drugs, is military in nature: to destroy the enemy quasi-state, the international drug trafficking interest, by destroying or confiscating that quasi-state's economic and financial resources, by disbanding business and political associations associated with the drug trafficking interest, by confiscating the wealth accumulated through complicity with the drug traffickers' operations, and by detaining, as "prisoners of war" or as traitors or spies, all persons aiding the drug trafficking interest...

- Special attention should be concentrated on those banks, insurance enterprises, and other business institutions which are in fact elements of an international financial cartel coordinating the flow of hundreds of billions annually of revenues from the international drug traffic. Such entities should be classed as outlaws according to the "crimes against humanity" doctrine elaborated at the postwar Nuremberg Tribunal, and all business relations with such entities should be prohibited according to the terms of prohibition against trading with the enemy in time of war...

- One of the worst problems we continue to face in combating drug trafficking, especially since political developments of the 1977-81 period, is the increasing corruption of governmental agencies and personnel, as well as influential political factions, by politically powerful financial interests associated with either the drug trafficking as such, or powerful financial and business interests associated with conduiting the revenues of the drug trafficking. For this and related reasons, ordinary law-enforcement methods of combating the drug traffic fail. In addition to corruption of governmental agencies, the drug traffickers are protected by the growth of powerful groups which advocate either legalization of the drug traffic, or which campaign more or less efficiently to prevent effective forms of enforcement of laws against the usage and trafficking in drugs. Investigation has shown that the associations engaged in such advocacy are political arms of the financial interests associated with the conduiting of revenues from the drug traffic, and that they are therefore to be treated in the manner Nazi-sympathizer operations were treated in the United States during World War II. ...

- The War on Drugs should include agreed provisions for allotment of confiscated billions of dollars of assets of the drug trafficking interests to beneficial purposes of economic development, in basic economic infrastructure, agriculture, and goods-producing industry. These measures should apply the right of sovereign states to taking title of the foreign as well as domestic holdings of their nationals, respecting the lawful obligations of those nationals to the state. The fact that ill-gotten gains are transferred to accounts in foreign banks, or real estate holdings in foreign nations, does not place those holdings beyond reach of recovery by the state of that national.

This, then, is a War on Drugs, as defined by an old soldier, a patriotic veteran of World War II. It is a war intended to save not only America, but to help other nations such as Mexico and Colombia, working as partners with the United States, to free themselves from drug slavery. It is not a "war of words": There will be casualties. It is not for the squeamish or faint-of-heart.

President Trump's Feb. 9 Executive Order[5]

In his Executive Order, titled, *Enforcing Federal Law with Respect to Transnational Criminal Organizations and Preventing International Trafficking*, President Trump begins by saying:

Transnational criminal organizations and subsidiary organizations, including transnational drug cartels, have spread throughout the Nation, threatening the safety of the United States and its citizens. These organizations derive revenue through widespread illegal conduct, including acts of violence and abuse that exhibit a wanton disregard for human life...

These groups are drivers of crime, corruption, violence, and misery. In particular, the traf-

_____
5. See: https://www.whitehouse.gov/the-press-office/2017/02/09/presidential-executive-order-enforcing-federal-law-respect-transnational

ficking by cartels of controlled substances has triggered a resurgence in deadly drug abuse and a corresponding rise in violent crime related to drugs. Likewise, the trafficking and smuggling of human beings by transnational criminal groups, risks creating a humanitarian crisis. These crimes, along with many others, are enriching and empowering these organizations to the detriment of the American people.

Homeland Security Secretary John Kelly

C-SPAN

A comprehensive and decisive approach is required to dismantle these organized crime syndicates and restore safety for the American people.

From there, the President goes on to define a new policy, aimed at strengthening "enforcement of Federal law in order to thwart transnational criminal organizations and subsidiary organizations, including criminal gangs, cartels, racketeering organizations, and other groups engaged in illicit activities that present a threat to public safety and national security, and that are related to, for example."

This will include, "the illegal smuggling and trafficking of humans, drugs or other substances, wildlife, and weapons"; as well as corruption, fraud and financial crimes, including "the illegal concealment or transfer of proceeds de-

Eli Alford for the Executive Office for U.S. Attorneys

Attorney General Jeff Sessions

rived from such illicit activities."

He defines a policy to "ensure that Federal law enforcement agencies give a high priority and devote sufficient resources to efforts to identify, interdict, disrupt, and dismantle transnational criminal organizations and subsidiary organizations, including through the investigation, apprehension, and prosecution of members of such organizations," as well as to "enhance cooperation with foreign counterparts against transnational criminal organizations and subsidiary organizations...," to "pursue and support additional efforts to prevent the operational success of transnational criminal organizations and subsidiary organizations within and beyond the United States, to include prosecution...," and to "work to increase intelligence and law enforcement information sharing with foreign partners battling transnational criminal organizations and subsidiary organizations, and to enhance international operational capabilities and cooperation," as well as to "assess Federal agencies' allocation of monetary and personnel resources for identifying, interdicting, and dismantling transnational criminal organizations and subsidiary organizations...," and to "identify Federal agencies' practices, any absence of practices, and funding needs that might hinder Federal efforts to effectively combat transnational criminal organizations and subsidiary organizations..."

The Executive Order directs the Attorney General and the Secretary of Homeland Security to report back to the President within 120 days, and to submit a report "on transnational criminal organizations and subsidiary organizations, including the extent of penetration of such organizations into the United States, and issue additional reports annually thereafter to describe the progress made in combating these criminal organizations, along with any recommended actions for dismantling them."

It is very clear that this initial action taken by President Trump does not go as far as what Lyndon LaRouche proposed in 1985. Yet, it also must be understood, that everything contained in that Order, issued under the authority of President Trump, is *fully coherent* with LaRouche's earlier proposal. This is the first step in the War.

IV. Victory

As Douglas MacArthur understood in Japan in 1945, to win the peace one must provide the people of a nation with a pathway to the future. Military victory must be followed by a long-term peace-winning vision.

On Nov. 29, 2016, Philippine President Rodrigo Duterte inaugurated the opening of the Mega Drug Abuse Treatment and Rehabilitation Center (Mega DATRC). Still incomplete, this facility when finished will be capable of housing 10,000 recovering drug addicts. In his Nov. 29 speech, President Duterte strongly reiterated his determination to win the drug war in the Philippines, and he stressed the importance of facilities such as Mega in furthering the reintegration of the victims of the drug cartels back into society.[6]

The tens of millions of drug users in the United States are the *victims* of Britain's modern Opium War against the United States. By adopting the measures which LaRouche enunciated in 1985, together with enactment of Glass-Steagall legislation as well as strict enforcement of federal drug laws, the amount of drug consumption can be drastically curtailed. The availability of drugs will be sharply reduced, and the message that has been sent out by Barack Obama for the last eight years that "Drugs are OK" will be reversed. A contrary social dynamic will be created. The question then becomes how to move forward, how to create a

better culture and a better society than that which currently exists.

How To Make the Victory Permanent: Taking A Page from Franklin Roosevelt

Between 1933 and 1937, four agencies created by Franklin Roosevelt—the Civilian Conservation Corps (CCC), the Federal Emergency Relief Administration (FERA), the Civil Works Administration (CWA), and the Works Progress Administration (WPA)—created more than ten million jobs, primarily for young Americans. The primary goal was to "put people back to work," but—beyond that urgent immediate need—it must also be stressed that many of these jobs created by FDR also involved building something which *improved the nation:*

- Bridges
- Schools
- Hospitals
- Dams
- Electrification.

A better future was being created, and the youth involved were part of this.

The effect of such a dynamic can not be underestimated.

During the recent Presidential campaign, Donald Trump spoke out often about his determination to rebuild America's inner cities. He told one audience of African-American voters in Detroit, "You're living in poverty, your schools are no good, you have no jobs, 58% of your youth are unemployed; what the hell do you have to lose?" He was ridiculed for making such statements and even, incredibly, called a racist by some in the media. Yet, it is precisely in the President's enunciation of his intent to rescue inner city dwellers, that the revelation for a permanent victory in the drug war begins to become clear.

Imagine if the Trump Administration were to establish dozens—if not hundreds—of facilities modeled on the Philippine Mega facility of President Duterte, and if those facilities were linked to a Franklin Roosevelt jobs program for rebuilding America's cities. Imagine if hundreds of thousands or even millions of such youth received training and were put to work rehabilitating and improving areas of the Bronx, Brooklyn, or the inner cities of Chicago, Baltimore, Detroit, and other major American metropolitan areas. What if the same thing were done in depressed rural areas. What would be the effect on the nation? The fleeting pleasures of

---

6. The full speech may be viewed at https://www.youtube.com/watch?v=2VZbTIM-ofM

drug intoxication might be replaced by tangible progress which promises a better future.

Even far greater challenges—and greater opportunities—could then be posed to young Americans. A true Hamiltonian economic policy will provide the means to take on stupendous projects, including a rapid return to space exploration, in partnership with other nations. An upward optimistic perspective can take hold. The potential for a profoundly positive change in culture would then become possible. Human minds begin to function again. Reason awakens. Cognition is improved.

Justice

There is no reason to incarcerate drug users. Again, they are the victims. Simply cut off their supply, and move as many of them as possible into an FDR economic recovery effort. This approach should also apply for many "lower level" individuals involved in the drug trade, if their crime is non-violent and their desire to escape the drug lifestyle is genuine. The only necessary caution is to avoid excessive leniency until the drug cartels are crushed.[7] Forgiveness after a war is laudable; during the war it is suicidal.

For those with serious problems of addiction or severe psychological problems, rehabilitation clinics should be the first step. According to a report by the U.S. Substance Abuse and Mental Health Services Administration (SAMHSA), almost 23 million Americans aged 12 and older need treatment for drug or alcohol use, but only 2.5 million have received treatment at a specialty facility.

For the controllers and the military command structure of Dope, Inc., no mercy must be permitted.

Leading bankers and financiers involved in drug money laundering or drug transactions, either directly or through connivance, should be stripped of their ill-gotten gains, prosecuted, and jailed. No one should be immune, including CEOs and others in executive positions. During their 2012 plea bargain, the top officials of HSBC openly admitted that they had knowingly laundered *billions* of dollars in drug money. Not one of them spent a day in jail.

All high level officials and major players in drug gangs and drug cartels should be similarly treated. This falls under the heading of "military procedures," and it will necessitate cooperation with a variety of other nations.

Any state or local government official, elected official, or law enforcement official who defies federal law in regard to the War on Drugs, i.e., commits treason, should be prosecuted to the fullest extent of the law. The issue of "states' rights" was settled on the bloody battlefields of Gettysburg and Shiloh. The same approach might be necessary for some within the nation's major news media.

Responsible individuals, again including top corporate officers within the Pharmaceutical industry, who have wittingly participated in the mass drugging of the American people, should be indicted and prosecuted. Procedures which govern the availability of powerful psychiatric drugs must be radically overhauled.

Such ruthless action will cripple the command structures of the enemy and destroy their ability to continue to operate. At the same time, it will accomplish a great shift in the morale of the American people. It is time to resurrect the methods of Ferdinand Pecora who jailed Wall Street bankers in the 1930s. If the CEOs of major financial institutions are marched in handcuffs off to prison, together with the leaders of the major drug cartels, everyone will know that this war is deadly serious.

In his 1985 Mexico City address, Lyndon LaRouche stated, "Special attention should be concentrated on those banks, insurance enterprises, and other business institutions which are in fact elements of an international financial cartel coordinating the flow of hundreds of billions annually of revenues from the international drug traffic. Such entities should be classed as outlaws according to the 'crimes against humanity' doctrine elaborated at the postwar Nuremberg Tribunal."

What LaRouche said then was true, and it remains true today.

---

7. Some individuals attack anti-drug prosecutions, pointing to what has been done to young African-American males during the last 20 to 30 years. As of 2017, it is estimated that one-third of black male Americans will spend time in state or federal prison at some point in their lifetime—more than double the rate from the 1970s. The majority of these incarcerations are for drug-related convictions, and the effect this has had on black families and the black community is both well known and devastating. Yet, what is less well known is that only about 14% of those convictions involved violent or property crimes; the vast bulk were for drug possession or even such things as the possession of "drug paraphernalia." These are precisely the type of people who should be directed toward a Duterte/FDR program.

Oroville Dam's Near Catastrophe: A Wake-Up Call for the Nation

by Patrick Ruckert

Feb. 26—Late Sunday afternoon on February 12, an emergency alarm was sounded by the Yuba County, California Sheriff:

> This is an evacuation order. Immediate evacuation from the low levels of Oroville and areas downstream is ordered. A hazardous situation is developing with the Oroville Dam auxiliary spillway. Operation of the auxiliary spillway has led to severe erosion that could lead to a failure of the structure. Failure of the auxiliary spillway structure will result in an uncontrolled release of flood waters from Lake Oroville. Immediate evacuation from the low levels of Oroville and areas downstream is ordered. This in *not a* Drill. This in *not a* Drill. This in *not a* Drill.

Soon, 188,000 people were in their cars, jamming the roads and becoming more and panic-stricken as authorities were warning over emergency broadcast networks that the Oroville Dam emergency spillway could collapse within the hour. Had it done so, a 30-foot wall of water would have swept down the valley of the Feather River. The casualties would have been in the thousands.

We shall return to the story of Oroville Dam shortly. But, first, to be blunt, the dams, the bridges, the roads—the entire infrastructure system of the nation, is not only inadequate, but it is falling apart after decades of neglect. Fifty years of the "post-industrial society," with the turning of our once-magnificent industrial, scientific, and infrastructure-driven economy into a nightmare of Wall Street financial speculation, has wrecked what was the most productive economy in the world.

This is not the place to catalog all the symptoms of this crime against humanity, but I want to use the near catastrophe of Oroville Dam to discuss the potential now represented by the Trump Presidency to, in his words, "make America great again." Neither dams nor nations can be made great by words alone. Those who wish to do so must know what they are doing and take the necessary action.

We shall begin by noting what President Donald Trump said last week, speaking at the Conservative PAC conference in Washington, D.C.:

> We've spent trillions of dollars overseas while allowing our own infrastructure to fall into total disrepair and decay. In the Middle East, we've spent as of four weeks ago $6 trillion. Think of

Tomruen/public domain

The I-35 bridge collapsed into the Mississippi River in Minneapolis, Minnesota on Aug. 1, 2007.

it. And, by the way, the Middle East is in what—I mean, it's not even close—it's in much worse shape than it was 15 years ago. If our Presidents would have gone to the beach for 15 years, we would be in much better shape than we are right now—that I can tell you. Yeah, a hell of a lot better. We could have rebuilt our country three times with that money.

The President is right, and he has put forth as his policy the investment of $1 trillion over ten years in building and rebuilding America's infrastructure. What he has not made clear is how even that moderate plan is to be done—moderate because one trillion over ten years does not even come close to what is required.

In an interview with editor Joseph Ford Cotto of the *San Francisco Review of Books*, published Feb. 15, 2017, Lyndon LaRouche said:

> Trump has promised to invest $1 trillion in urgently needed infrastructure and promised the implementation of a 21st-century Glass Steagall Act. If he implements his infrastructure promise, he will need that reform to finance it.... Really we're talking about Trump on the basis that he is now the new leader for the United States. He has promised to build up the American economy again, and there are great precedents of American presidents using the American System of Economy as it was developed by Alexander Hamilton, explicitly in contrast to the British System of Free Trade. That is the system that worked in the past, and it will work again. Now, what Trump has done by his success, here, is to build up the possibility of a revival of the U.S. economy.

U.S. Infrastructure Flunks the Test

Though the term infrastructure is used here, a word of context must be stated. Some years ago, Lyndon LaRouche made the point that the term *infrastructure* is inadequate; it does not describe the real process of human progress. Rather, the term *platforms of productivity* should be used to represent how mankind's economy must always be governed by a process of leaping upward in its productive power. It is by introducing new scientific principles, and applying those discoveries through new technologies, that our species is able to increase its *potential relative population density*, also a term created by LaRouche. New platforms of produc-

tivity transform the entire array of technologies of an economy, much like the introduction of railroads did in the 19th Century, and the Apollo Project did in the 1960s.

The American Society of Civil Engineers regularly issues a Report Card, rating the various categories of our nation's infrastructure. The Report Card for 2013 tells us that if the nation were a student we would be repeating the second grade. The price tag, as estimated by the Society, *just to repair the existing infrastructure* by 2020, is $3.6 trillion. Thousands of dams and bridges need repair, many of which are in a dangerous condition. The five-year California drought was alleviated by a dramatic increase of pumping groundwater from the aquifers, which has created a subsidence of the ground throughout especially the Central Valley. As the ground subsides, damage to roadways, bridges, and even the California Aqueduct, is now occurring and will cost tens of millions to repair. For just California alone, the "report card" specifies $65 billion per year is required to fix and maintain its water infrastructure. And that does not include the $1 billion in damage to the roads and bridges of the state caused by the past few weeks of flooding.

Case Study: U.S. Dams

The following excerpts from the Report Card of the American Society of Civil Engineers summarize the numbers, the conditions, and the cost immediately required to ensure the safety of U.S. dams:

Thousands of our nation's dams are in need of rehabilitation to meet current design and safety standards. They are not only aging, but are subject to stricter criteria as a result of increased downstream development and advancing scientific knowledge predicting flooding, earthquakes, and dam failures.

The average age of the 84,000 dams in the country is 52 years. The nation's dams are aging, and the number of high-hazard dams is on the rise. Many of these dams were built as low-hazard dams protecting undeveloped agricultural land. However, with an increasing population and greater development below dams, the overall number of high-hazard dams continues to increase, to nearly 14,000 in 2012. The number of deficient dams is estimated at more than 4,000, which includes 2,000 deficient high-hazard dams. The Association of State Dam Safety Officials estimates that it will require an investment of $21 billion to repair these aging, yet critical, high-hazard dams.

The complexity of monitoring the conditions of our

nation's dams arises partly because they are owned and operated by many different entities. While some of the nation's dams are owned and operated by federal, state, and local governments, the majority, 69%, are owned by a private entity. The federal government owns 3,225 dams, or approximately 4% of the nation's dams. It may be surprising to some that the U.S. Army Corps of Engineers owns only 694 dams.

Other than 2,600 dams regulated by the Federal Energy Regulatory Commission, the remaining dams in the nation are not regulated by the federal government, but instead rely on state dam safety programs for inspection. State dam safety programs have primary responsibility and permitting, inspection, and enforcement authority for 80% of the nation's dams.

William Croyle, California Dept. of Water Resources

An official Feb. 17, 2017 photo showing the damaged spillway that has eroded the hillside in Oroville.

Funding needs are significant, and vary according to who owns and operates the dam. The Association of State Dam Safety Officials estimates that the total cost to rehabilitate the nation's non-federal and federal dams is over $57 billion. To rehabilitate just those dams categorized as most critical, or high-hazard, would cost the nation $21 billion, a cost that continues to rise as maintenance, repair, and rehabilitation are delayed. Overall, state dam safety program staffing has increased over the past several years. However, in 2011 state programs spent over $44 million on their regulatory programs, a decrease from recent years.

The U.S. Army Corps of Engineers estimates that more than $25 billion will be required to address dam deficiencies for Corps-owned dams.

The Oroville Dam

Oroville Dam is just one of thousands of dams in the nation that forty years of neglect have made dangerous to millions of people. Oroville Dam must be the wake-up call to the nation that a serious infrastructure building and repair policy must be initiated now.

Oroville Dam is not only the tallest dam in the United States at 770 feet, but it is the lynch-pin reservoir of the California State Water Project, which, with the Central Valley Project initiated by FDR, created the most extensive and complex water management system

in the world. The dam is about 80 miles northeast of Sacramento and sits on the Feather River, which flows into the Sacramento River, and is the heart of the system that provides the water for 23 million people and millions of acres of farmland, including southern California, 400 miles to the south.

It is an earthen dam with a concrete core and was completed in 1968. For fifty years the emergency spillway had never been used until, suddenly in early February, the regular spillway began to disintegrate. The emergency spillway was never armored with concrete and thus remained nothing but a hill of dirt sitting under the berm of concrete to the west of the dam itself. Warnings were made twelve years ago that, should the emergency spillway be required to be used, the dirt below the berm would rapidly wash away and the foundation of the berm would collapse. These warnings were dismissed by both state and federal regulators as an improbable danger. In truth, armoring the spillway would have cost some millions in 1968, and probably ten times that in 2005, which neither the Bush nor the Schwarzenegger administration, nor the water contractors who would have had to cover some of the cost, wanted to bear.

When the main spillway began to disintegrate on Feb. 7, the decision to close the gates to the spillway was made, and the gates were closed on Feb. 10. Stopping the flow down the spillway, with more than

100,000 cubic feet of water flowing per second into the reservoir from the storm run-off and melting snow, resulted in the reservoir level rising as much as 10 feet per day. On Feb. 11, the rising reservoir overflowed into the emergency spillway, while at the same time water was once again allowed to flow down the main spillway, as the managers accepted the consequence that still more damage would be done to it.

The emergency spillway, the designers and engineers claimed, would be able to handle a flow of 250,000 cubic feet of water per minute (cfm). On Sunday afternoon, Feb. 12, with a flow of just over 12,000 cfm, it became clear that the water was eroding the hillside, threatening a collapse of the berm that would send a wall of water 30 feet high down the river and into the communities below. That is when the emergency evacuation order was issued. The regular spillway's gates were immediately reopened, and within a day the water level in the reservoir had fallen below the lip of the berm, stopping the flow of water down the emergency spillway. Two days later people were given the all-clear signal to return to their homes.

In the two weeks since, the regular spillway has remained opened, and the reservoir level is now 50 feet below the top of the dam. Further damage to the regular spillway is assumed to be occurring, but for now, access to it is impossible due to the high-volume flow of water. The early estimate of the cost to repair the spillway, which won't be possible to do until the winter and spring run-off subsides, is $200 million.

China Offers to Help Make America Great

In January of this year, Ding Xuedong, the chairman of the China Investment Corporation (CIC), offered to change the CIC's holdings of U.S. Treasury debt, into an investment for the building of new infrastructure in the United States. Ding's estimate of the investment needed to build a new and modern economic infrastructure in America was a very large $8 trillion. CIC now holds $50 billion in U.S. Treasuries, a part of $1.14 trillion in Treasuries held by Chinese institutions. The insane "quantitative easing" policy of the Federal Reserve has made the returns on those Treasury bills virtually zero. The Chinese would like a better return on their holdings, and see investing in building U.S. infrastructure as a way to do so. In addition, of course, that opens the door to more U.S.-Chinese cooperation. This is a reflection of the *Win-Win* strategy of President Xi's One Belt One Road policy, or as it is often referred to— "The New Silk Road." In addition to these Chinese pro-posals, it must also be mentioned that Japanese Prime Minister Abe, in his discussions with President Trump earlier this month, also offered to invest one to two trillion dollars in U.S. infrastructure.

The vehicle for investment in U.S. infrastructure that the CIC is seeking, in fact, does not yet exist; it would be a "Hamiltonian" national credit institution for infrastructure and manufacturing investments, as specified in *EIR* Founding Editor Lyndon LaRouche's "Four Laws to Save the United States Economy" in 2014.

These *Four Laws* start with reimposing Franklin Roosevelt's Glass-Steagall legislation, together with a return to Hamiltonian National Banking as a means of extending credit into the real economy, spearheaded by science drivers in fusion energy development and a restoration of NASA and the exploration of space.

In 2014, Lyndon LaRouche's political action committee, LaRouche PAC, published a detailed report on exactly what the U.S. policy must be. That report, "The United States Joins the New Silk Road: A Hamiltonian Vision for an Economic Renaissance," soon to be updated, provides the blueprint President Trump must adopt. The plan includes:

• A nationwide high-speed and maglev rail network;

• Connecting North America to Asia via a Bering Strait Tunnel;

• The building of new Renaissance cities with a mission to drive forward the frontiers of science;

• The rapid development of fusion energy;

• An expanded space program; and

• Great water projects to manage the global water cycle.

Last week, the President met with about 30 leaders of American industrial corporations, and he was informed by them of the problems their companies are having in getting financing to expand production and to increase their exports, incuding, for example, the virtual cut-off of guarantees from the U.S. Export-Import Bank.

For American corporations, the export market means life or death. For example, General Motors delivered a record 3,870,587 vehicles to China in 2016, and China remained GM's largest market in terms of retail sales for the fifth consecutive year, accounting for more than one-third of the company's global sales. Similarly, Caterpillar, Inc, the world's largest producer of heavy machinery, saw its sales fall in 2016, except to China, where expanded sales are driven by China's massive infrastructure-building as part of the One Belt One Road policy.

III. Day of Truth—Obama's Ukraine Coup

A MOMENT FOR GREATNESS

International Day of Truth Exposes British Empire/Soros Hand in Ukraine And U.S. Color Revolutions

by Diane Sare

Feb. 27—On Thursday, Feb. 23, on the third anniversary of the Nazi coup in the Ukraine, activists associated with the LaRouche political movement deployed to get out the truth around the globe—and emphatically in the United States, itself—as to what happened in the Ukraine in 2014 and how, today, the very same forces and methods are being hurled against U.S. President Donald Trump.

The Feb. 23 mobilization was powerful enough that it has already elicited howls of hysteria from former Nazi-collaborator and Queen Elizabeth II-moneybags George Soros, who has denied "any direct connection to the [allegedly] growing tide of anti-Trump demonstrators." Additionally, as the on-the-ground reports given below indicate, the majority of Americans are not, in fact, being whipped up into an anti-Trump hysteria, as the news media would have you believe, but rather are searching for answers and are remarkably open to reasoned discussion.

Approximately three weeks ago, founder of the Schiller Institutes and Chairwoman of the German Schiller Institute, Helga Zepp-LaRouche, called for an international "Day of Truth" on the occasion of the third anniversary of the British Empire's "color revolution" coup in Ukraine. This proposed action was especially necessary because the very same interests which overthrew the democratically elected Yanukovych government in Ukraine, replacing it with a pro-Nazi regime of terror, have now resurrected their anti-Russian lies from that period, to attempt to overthrow the newly elected American President. (See Jan. 21, 2017 *London Spectator,* "Will Donald Trump be assassinated, ousted

EIRNS/Sylvia Spaniolo
New York City LaRouche PAC Ukraine Mobilization, in Union Square, Feb. 24, 2017.

in a coup or just impeached?")

On Feb. 13, President Trump's National Security Advisor, Michael Flynn, was forced to resign over his contact with diplomatic representatives of the Russian Federation. The "failing" *New York Times,* as President Trump rightly calls it, had a feature article accusing at least four of Trump's inner circle of having "illicit contact" with the Russian Federation. As you will read in the reports below, most Americans agree with President Trump's efforts for a dialogue with Russia as a critical initiative that is preferable to war between two nuclear powers, and the media hype about Russia is actually causing people to become curious about what is really going on. It is the task of the LaRouche Movement worldwide to expose the truth of the matter, and put an end to this dangerous geopolitical threat of thermonuclear war once and for all.

To this end, last week, *Executive Intelligence Review* published a 17-page dossier for mass circulation, both in the United States and worldwide. The dossier, titled "Obama and Soros—Nazis in Ukraine 2014—U.S. in 2017?" has been circulated electronically and at highly visible rallies and street corners in the following cities: Berlin and Dresden, Germany; Copenhagen, Denmark; Montreal, Canada; Stockholm, Sweden; Mexico City and Hermosillo, Mexico; Guatemala City; Buenos Aires, Argentina; Santo Domingo, Dominican Republic; Caracas, Venezuela; Cali, Colombia; Madrid, Spain; as well as Houston, Boston, Seattle, Washington, D.C., New York City, and other cities in the United States.

On the *Day of Truth*, the center of the activity in the United States was Manhattan, where activists held a rally near the United Nations and distributed copies of the dossier to diplomats and institutional representatives. Over 70 copies were given to diplomats from two dozen countries or more, as well as to individuals with various UN agencies. Over 200 copies of the *Hamiltonian* broadsheet, "The Voice of the LaRouche Political Movement," were also distributed at this location, and the rally and distribution of the report were covered in the Russian wire service TASS, as well as in *Sputnik News* in several different languages.

Press coverage particularly featured the signs calling for jailing both Soros and Obama for treason, as well as material from the dossier about Victoria Nuland's boast of the U.S. State Department's expenditure of $5 billion to more than 2,000 NGOs in Ukraine, many affiliated with Soros's Open Society Institute. Both Sputnik and Tass also made prominent mention of

Sputnik News *reporting the LaRouche PAC Day of Truth campaign, exposing the truth on the 2014 coup in Ukraine.*

the recent Schiller Institute Chorus memorials to the Alexandrov Ensemble.

At the UN deployment, passers-by were generally very open, with only a pitifully small handful of "Hillary screamers," still trying to convince themselves that Russia hacked the election. One young African-American veteran said that he had been surprised by the barrage of media attacks on Trump, since Trump is "white and rich." So he figured that the President must be up to something that the establishment is afraid of. He stuck around to talk and observe for several minutes. Cars with diplomatic plates were observed stopping in front of the rally with their windows open to hear the briefing, and many people came back after reading the material, to ask questions and get more information.

EIRNS/Sylvia Spaniolo

LaRouche PAC Day of Truth organizing at Union Square, New York City, Feb. 24, 2017.

Rationality Awakens

In addition to this report from New York City, initial reports from our International Day of Truth as well as from other recent political events, show Americans and others responding to us in unexpectedly rational and sensible ways, often with deep and wide-ranging impromptu discussions. And this is regardless of political label.

During the seven days, LaRouche activists have participated in at least eight Congressional Town Hall meetings in Los Angeles and the San Francisco Bay Area. All but one of these were in Democratic districts, districts which voted overwhelmingly for Hillary Clinton in the recent election. These were extraordinary meetings, with attendance at many in the range of 800 to 1,000 people, whereas most Congressional meetings from the recent past drew well under one hundred.

What characterized almost all of these meetings was a great deal of fear and uncertainty—expressed by many of the speakers in the form that they "don't know what the future might bring"—but also an overriding civility and a noticeable lack of anti-Trump rhetoric. These were most emphatically not "leftist Tea Party" events.

For example, at one of the meetings, a district in Silicon Valley which voted 83 percent to 17 percent for Democratic Congressional candidates in last year's primaries, almost all of the questions were about health care, immigration (many Asians live in this district), science policy, Social Security, and infrastructure. Rather than attacking Trump, most of the speakers wanted to know what the Congressman personally was going to do about these issues, and at one point, the Democratic Congressman even invited Trump supporters in the audience to speak up. A few of the meetings were somewhat more polarized, but nowhere did anyone demand Trump's removal from office, and at all of the meetings what people clearly expressed is that what they are most concerned with are solutions for these problems.

In Boston, former Congressman Dennis Kucinich gave a speech at Harvard sponsored by a Massachusetts Peace Action-affiliated Harvard student group. Attendance included anti-war activists, former Kucinich activists, and Harvard students—just the type of audience which the *New York Times* desires to mobilize against President Trump. Kucinich delivered a powerful address, stressing the message which he has most recently focused on: That there is no reason for war with Russia, and that especially the left should not get duped into supporting such a war.

Kucinich repeatedly attacked Barack Obama by name. He talked about his own visits to Russia in the 90's, and the humanity of the Russian people and culture, which are deeply affected by the loss of thirty million people in World War II. He said that he had read the DNI report on purported Russian interference in the election, that it was "pretty sketchy" and that the validity of the charge of DNC hacking is "still open." He brought up Obama's request for $1 trillion for upgrading the nuclear arsenal, the U.S. missile defense shield, and the expansion of NATO to Russia's border. He said that these actions, combined with the continual hostile rhetoric, are creating a "witches brew for a new Cold War," which is very dangerous.

He also quoted—positively—from Trump's speech earlier that day about the mistakes in the Middle East, where the President said that we could have rebuilt the United States with all of that money. Kucinich harshly criticized Obama a number of times, for putting troops in Syria, for working with a "bad array of people" there, and for his drone-kill sessions where Obama picked his targets from "baseball cards."

LaRouche PAC organizers in attendance asked two questions: the first on the Ukraine coup, and the role of Victoria Nuland and Soros; and the second on the connection between what was done three years ago in the Ukraine, and what is being orchestrated now in the United States to bring down President Trump.

Kucinich responded very seriously by emphatically describing the "U.S. coup" in Ukraine, detailing Victoria Nuland's role—after the previous Ukraine government had refused to sign an economic agreement that was against their own interests. He said that the United States makes "cars, planes, and coups," and if it smells like a coup, don't be surprised, because that's what we do. On the second part, he said Trump was democratically elected; the election was not stolen, it was constitutional; and it is not lawful to attempt to oust the government. LaRouche PAC literature was given to most of the participants, who were all happy to receive it.

EIRNS/Rachel Brown

LaRouche PAC Day of Truth organizing in Boston, Mass., Feb. 24, 2017.

The Day of Truth

In addition to the Manhattan deployments reported above, the Day of Truth also witnessed rallies, interventions, and other activity in a variety of American cities. What follows is a handful of reports from a few of them.

Seattle: Three organizers made a banner titled "Jail Obama and Soros for Treason, Ukraine 2014 USA 2017." In the early morning rush hour, the banner was displayed from a freeway overpass just off the exit for the University of Washington. To the surprise of the organizers, the ratio of supporting honking and middle fingers was 50:50. So much for the "liberal" majority of Seattle!

As the organizers reported, "After morning rush hour, we then hit the University of Washington with the truth. With banner raised and tables set, we were swamped with students for quite a while—mostly students who were very confused about what was going on. Notable was an increase in students who would tell us that they have been thinking that something was fishy about the media, and that they knew something was "off." These students were not Trump supporters or Hillary/Obama supporters, but genuinely confused, given all the media garbage. They were thankful for the briefing, and some left contact information or sat down to talk. There were international students who would defend us from "narratives," including one from Azerbaijan who made it very clear to other students that Russia never invaded Ukraine, and that it was actually the Nazis who were provoking "both sides to shoot each other."

In the evening rush hour, the response to the overpass banner was even more enthusiastic: "We had bus drivers, laborers, cleaning ladies, truckers, and even police officers honking and giving thumbs up! It definitely seemed to be more lively this time around, and to be more for us than against us. We also noticed that it had a remoralizing effect when one person honked, and that would set off a chain of others who probably had been scared to show their excitement."

Houston: Members and activists of the LaRouche political movement in Houston held a highway overpass rally, with the same banner as described above. A conversation between our activists and the police officers who were there to protect the rally, revealed that a younger officer had been scheduled to be part of the training offered by the Obama Administration to the Kiev government. He was sent to Kiev; but he, at least, was not involved in a program there. He was a bit shocked to learn the full story, but the Soros involvement was not surprising to him, as he had been following reports of Soros' involvement in "Black Lives Matter."

The support from passing cars was largely positive, with many drivers honking and giving "thumbs up." Later, a few people went into the downtown tunnels and found a very open and inquisitive response from people who knew that something was behind the anti-Russia hype, but were not sure what it was. People wanted to know the truth about Ukraine, and the U.S. support

EIRNS/Sylvia Spaniolo

Day of Truth Ukraine Mobilization in Union Square, New York City, Feb. 24, 2017.

behind the coup under Obama. They wanted to know what was setting off the anti-Trump and anti-Russia insanity in the United States, and what were the operations behind the demonstrations. One African-American who walked past our team and then came back, said "Soros works for the Rothschilds." Another tweener who stopped to take literature, had been reading LaRouche for some time. A young woman who stopped with four friends, said "Soros has to be stopped."

Washington, D.C.: Five activists armed with seven large signs and a table set up at Dupont Circle, which is the intersection of the streets housing most of the foreign embassies to the United States, as well as most of the so-called "think tanks" About one hundred copies of the Hamiltonian and the leaflet "Are the Same People who lied to you about Ukraine…" were distributed to passers-by.

From the organizers: "There were a number of freakouts from the Obama/Clinton crowd, probably from the nearby Brookings Institution. A couple of Clinton supporters screamed obscenities, but they were just being their eloquent selves. There was subdued

support for Trump, but the most polarizing sign was clearly 'No War with Russia, Putin is Your Friend.' One train worker, as well as a sanitation worker who has followed LaRouche for a long time, were very happy to see us out organizing. There were also several immigrants, a half a dozen or so who were *strong* Trump supporters, which seems to be a consistent pattern in the Maryland area."

All the members of the Senate Foreign Relations Committee received the Ukraine dossier in their Washington offices, as did other Senators totalling over 30 members of the Senate. All 45 members of the House Foreign Relations Committee will get it on March 1.

Boston: There was an early morning leaflet distribution downtown, including a car decorated with signs about the Soros-Obama coup, and "Russia is not your enemy, Wall Street is," as well as signs for Glass-Steagall. One team stayed in Boston for the day, and others went to a transit stop in Quincy.

From the organizers: Many people had a sense of the coup, or were willing to take the flyer who we didn't think would do so. A few people came back to get literature. One said, "I'm glad there are some sane people out there." A young twenty-something guy pulled out his earbuds, came over, and said, "That whole mess in Ukraine is our fault; the United States did that." Another man in his sixties signed up and said, "God bless you for being out here; I have to applaud your courage." He was familiar with LaRouche. A young man from Brazil, said, "This happened to us in Brazil! You're right!" There was also a minority of Soros-oriented people who would angrily refuse to take the leaflet.

At the table deployment in Boston, a woman in her early thirties said that Russia was not the enemy, but Wall Street is the problem. She was against Trump, and has been to all of the anti-Trump rallies, but she stayed to engage in discussion. She was challenged not just to resist, but to have a solution, and she gave her contact information to stay in touch. Another younger man who does environmental canvassing in Chicago, joined LaRouche PAC with a membership contribution, saying he agreed on stopping Wall Street's policy of perpetual war.

At the afternoon Quincy distribution a man pulled over and initially asked if we were working with the "Bernie people." When he was informed that we were with LaRouche, he said that he remembered LaRouche from the 1970s, and LaRouche's proposing a NASA-style budget for fusion,—something that he has always appreciated because he is a scientist.

New Revelations on Maidan Murders: A Plea to President Trump

by Bill Roberts

Feb. 26—Former Ukrainian President Victor Yanukovych and former Prime Minister Mykola Azarov, the key figures driven from power by the fascist Maidan Coup of late February 2014, have now dramatically revealed new details about the authorship of the sniper murders during the coup, and are proposing a truth commission to finally shatter the false narrative blaming Yanukovych for the escalation of Maidan violence.

This parallels the call several weeks ago by Helga Zepp-LaRouche, designating Feb. 23, 2017 as an international "Day of Truth" to expose the Obama/George Soros authorship of both the actually-Nazi "color revolution" that overthrew the Yanukovych government of Ukraine three years ago, as well as the clear present intention by those same actors to bring down the Trump Presidency in the United States. As detailed in the February 17, 20017 *EIR* special dossier "Obama and Soros—Nazis in Ukraine 2014—U.S. in 2017?" the Ukraine coup of February 2014 was an Anglo-American intelligence operation financed by Obama's State Department, organized to destroy the legitimately elected government of Yanukovych and lay the basis for war between Russia and the West.

On Feb. 21, in a post to his facebook page as reported by *Sputnik News*, former Ukraine Prime Minister Mykola Azarov dropped a bombshell, producing details about the identities of the snipers who sparked violence in the Maidan when they fired on both police and protesters, killing at least 50 people.

"Today we, and investigators in Kiev as well, have reliable information about the fact that the murders on the Maidan were carried out by special groups of snipers from Georgia, the Baltic countries, and Poland, under the guidance of instructors from France and Germany," Azarov writes. Azarov added that these groups "were provided with cover and diversionary actions by shooters from the 'Maidan Self-Defense' group under the direction of [Andriy] Parubiy and [Serhiy] Pashinsky," the former now serving as speaker of Ukraine's parliament, and the latter an MP and former interim head of the presidential administration. In total, more than 130 people, including 18 police officers, were killed.

Azarov explained that "the Georgian group, consisting of 10 people, was placed in the Conservatory building [which overlooks Maidan Square]. The identities of three of them have been confirmed by photographs taken by Ukrainian Security Forces staff, and it has been established that they are Georgian nationals. On February 20, [2014] this group divided into two. One of

Sputnik News *reports former Ukrainian Prime Minister Azarov's explosive revelations, Feb. 22, 2017.*

them fired from the conservatory building, the other from the Hotel Ukraine building." Azarov reports that the presence of a third group of shooters is assumed. This group reportedly killed 50 people in the space of 30 minutes from a third building overlooking the square, and were immediately moved out of the area.

Azarov notes that the coup plotters, Parubiy, Pashinskiy, Secretary of the National Defense Council Oleksander Turchynov, Interior Minister Arsen Avakov, and former prime minister Arseny Yatsenyuk, all of whom were appointed to their positions after the coup, "have done everything they could to destroy evidence and people's testimony. An attempt was made to place the blame for the massacre squarely on Yanukovych and the Berkut riot police."

Azarov's facebook posting contains many links to what appear to be eyewitness accounts from the Maidan, and numerous videos and photos documenting the violence on the Maidan in February 2014. The evidence exists, he says, that helps "establish with absolute objectivity" the involvement of Turchynov, Parubiy, Pashinsky, et al. in the organization of the mass carnage which took place three years ago.

One video shows Pashinsky stopped at a checkpoint on streets of central Kiev in February 2014 with a sniper rifle in the trunk of his car, which he recently claimed he was carrying for self-defense.

Earlier Evidence

This is not the first time it has been reported that the killers in Kiev were hired snipers. Not long after the murders, a conversation was leaked between Estonian Foreign Minister Urmas Paet and Katherine Ashton, foreign affairs chief of the EU, in which Paet told Ashton that the same snipers had killed both police and protesters, and that "somebody" from the "new ruling coalition" was behind them.

The day following Azarov's revelation, former Ukrainian President Victor Yanukovych called on the Council of Europe to convene an independent commission to investigate the coup event and murders in Ukraine from Feb. 18-22, 2014. He made the proposal in a letter to Chancellor Merkel and Foreign Minister Steinmeier of Germany, to the Presidents of France and Poland, as well as to the heads of the Council of Europe, the Parliamentary Assembly of the Council of Europe (PACE), and the European Parliament.

In a separate letter to President Trump, along with his call to investigate Maidan crimes, he called upon the U.S. President to "investigate the part played in them by U.S. officials" in backing the opposition, citing the role played in particular by then-U.S. Assistant Secretary of State for European and Eurasian Affairs Victoria Nuland, U.S. Senator John McCain, and then-U.S. Ambassador Geoffrey Pyatt. He also called on Trump to help bring an end to the bloodshed in Ukraine, a conflict which he said had resumed anew in the Donbass region after an offensive by the Kiev government in violation of the Minsk II agreements.

Speaking to a group of Russian and Ukrainian reporters in Moscow on the necessity for a truth commission, Yanukovych said:

> There are many witnesses who do not want to testify to the current authorities, do not want to provide any information, because they know that in the past three years all the evidence that could be destroyed, was destroyed. There are people who are willing to testify, but only to an international monitoring commission that should be set up in order to fulfill the agreement signed on February 21 [2014], and should particularly include representatives of the opposition and international experts.

He also charged that the current Ukrainian Prosecutor General, Yuri Lutsenko, had organized illegal activities and killings that took place at the Maidan, and had publicly said that the Maidan activists had weapons and were ready to use them.

"We are talking about the killings of innocent people who were shot dead from the buildings occupied by the Maidan activists," Yanukovich went on to say, according to TASS.

> Not one member of the Pravy Sektor [Right Sector] was killed; they were shooting ordinary people who had just come to the Maidan. Those people were in the area that was easy to target from the buildings where the snipers were. There are many proofs and people who are ready to testify.
>
> If the world community wants to know the truth and is willing to fulfill the pledges made before [when the February 21, 2014 agreement was signed], then all the criminals will be identified.

In response to these dramatic new revelations, Helga Zepp-LaRouche said, "This is something Trump should act on and it's something that would make Merkel and Steinmeier look very bad if they do not act on it."

IV. Obama's Genocide in Yemen

MESSAGE OF HELGA ZEPP-LAROUCHE

To the Berlin Conference on 'The Forgotten War Crimes in Yemen'

To the Participants in the Berlin Conference on "The Forgotten War Crimes in Yemen," Feb. 25, 2017

The war against Yemen, which the Saudi Arabian-led coalition and the United States have supported in many ways, has killed 10,000 people over the past two years, and now threatens the lives of more than twelve million who have been totally cut off from sustenance and medical supplies due to the systematic bombardment of the country's agricultural infrastructure, and the air and sea blockade. This war, by the official definition of the United Nations, is a genocide.

There is no case which better exemplifies the insufferable hypocrisy of the so-called "free West," than the lack of reporting on the war crimes which have been committed on a daily basis against the population of Yemen for the past two years. Where are all the advocates of "humanitarian intervention," who, under the pretext of defense of human rights, have incited one war after another on the basis of lies? Where is the coverage of the bombardments of funerals and hospitals, of the use of cluster bombs banned under international law, of the deaths of over a thousand children per week who are dying of preventable diseases? Where is the outcry about the systematic destruction of mankind's magnificent cultural heritage?

In the age of the Internet and NSA surveillance, no one can claim that the atrocities against the Yemeni population are not known to every government and all mass media. The decision to maintain de facto silence about them, only because the deeds are being carried out by "allies," makes them complicit in these crimes.

It is good that the new American Secretary of State

Helga Zepp-LaRouche addressing the Berlin conference on Yemen, via video link.

Rex Tillerson has promised "unfettered delivery of humanitarian assistance throughout Yemen." But there must be immediate international pressure exerted to end the war against Yemen right away, to rebuild the country, and to restore the destroyed cultural artifacts as much as possible.

One source of hope and consolation for the people of Yemen should be the fact that the BRICS countries and China's New Silk Road Initiative have made possible the prospect for confronting these challenges. The hopeful signs that a growing number of countries recognize the advantages of "win-win" cooperation, and are ready to break with geopolitics, also mean that the strategic situation for Yemen can soon improve.

In the meantime, everyone is called upon to support the appeal of the Yemeni people for an end to the war, and to direct the attention of the world to this very important and culturally rich country!

—Helga Zepp-LaRouche,
President of the international Schiller Institutes

Conference in Berlin—Crimes of The Forgotten War in Yemen

by Stefan Tolksdorf

Feb. 27—Under the above headline, an initiative of Yemeni citizens in Germany organized a conference on Saturday, February 25 in Berlin, to expose and to put an end to what is clearly an ongoing genocide against the people of Yemen. Two representatives of the international Schiller Institute, Elke Fimmen and Stefan Tolksdorf, were invited to participate. The following is a condensed report on the conference proceedings.

After the Yemeni national anthem and a beautiful recitation from the Quran, Mr. Abdullatif Elwashali stated in his introduction that Yemen is suffering from a full blockade by a Saudi-led coalition; the country's food supply is inadequate; schools and hospitals are being bombarded by modern fighter jets with precision targeting systems; and the country's vital ports are affected as well. The civilian population is suffering while the world remains silent, which is why the war is called "the forgotten war." This conference was intended to change that, and remind both the participants and the world of the victims of that war.

Dr. Werner Daum, a retired former German diplomat, was the first speaker. He has lived in Yemen for six years and is very familiar with the Yemeni people. "No people has touched me like the people of Yemen; their openness, their pride in their country without any arrogance, their securely resting in themselves." He stated that the Nuremberg Trials dealt with the question of wars of aggression. Ever since 1945, an unjustified war of aggression is a war crime, punishable by death. This is true today in Yemen. This war is unjustified; those responsible in Saudi Arabia and the Emirates are war criminals. He also pointed out that while the killing of people is already a terrible tragedy, the destruction of Yemen's cultural heritage is even worse, because it is irreplaceable.

Dr. Daum stressed that there is not a shred of proof for the false narrative that the war in Yemen is a conflict between Saudi Arabia and Iran. Any Iranian involvement is pure invention, a lie. "Yet, when the truth is no longer reported, this is because the freedom of the press is no longer guaranteed; not because some dictatorial

http://www.althwranews.net/

Feb. 25, 2017 coverage in Al-Thawra News *in Sana'a, Yemen, of the Berlin conference on "The Forgotten War Crimes in Yemen."*

Destroyed water utility in Abbs, Hajjah, Yemen.

regime is suppressing it, but because there exists a climate in this world in which only one truth is allowed to exist." He explicitly attacked Francis Fukuyama's fraudulent claim of the "end of history," and expressed his hope that this conference would help to unveil the truth about the terrible crimes being committed in Yemen today.

For the next keynote section, Elke Fimmen and Stefan Tolksdorf were invited to read a message to the conference by the President of the International Schiller Institute, Mrs. Helga Zepp-LaRouche, and to present the Schiller Institute's optimistic outlook and solution, and the fight the institute is leading internationally for a new paradigm, especially in the U.S.A. Besides confirming the absolute horror taking place in Yemen, Mrs. Fimmen briefed the audience on the political fight around the release of the 28 pages and the JASTA bill in the U.S.A. She outlined the beautiful perspective of developing Yemen as a Silk Road bridge between Asia and Africa, and presented the resolution that had been adopted at last June's Schiller Institute conference in Berlin, inspired by Fouad Al-Ghaffari's work in Yemen, and complemented it with a short slide show, prepared by Ulf Sandmark and Hussein Askary.

The conference organizers then presented some of the video evidence which they have gathered and produced as a "Crimes of the Forgotten War" DVD. After seeing the horrifying and heartbreaking images of death and destruction, Mr. Elwashali stressed that these crimes must be stopped immediately.

Hussain Sharaf then spoke on the subject of hope, poetically introducing the story of a young Yemeni girl, Amal, who loved airplanes and dreamed of flying and getting to know people all over the world. While on the street, looking at the airplanes which she heard coming, her house is hit by a bomb. He father dies immedi-

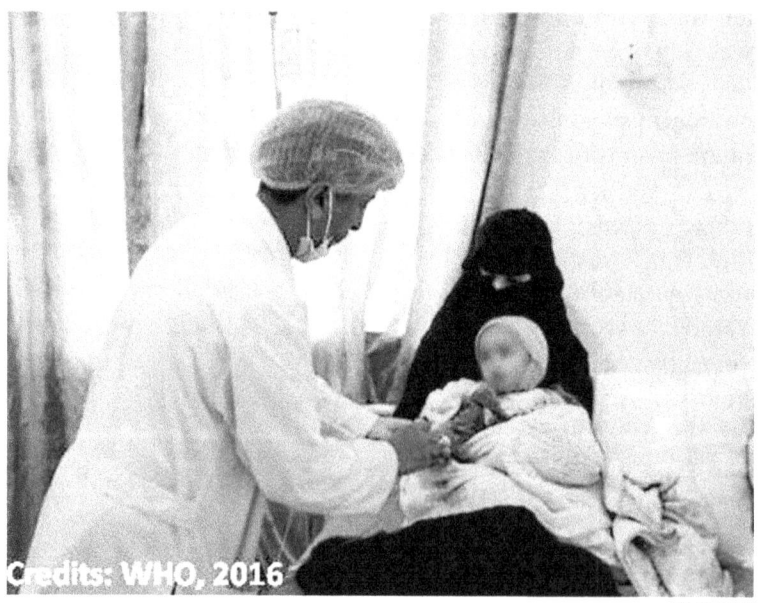

WHO, 2016

Child being treated for colera in Yemen.

ately—her mother and her younger brother were to die in a hospital without electricity soon after that. She lost all the light of her life and the great future that lay ahead of her. Though she was full of love, her body, her family, her soul and her dignity were injured. Amal means "hope," and hope is still alive and wants to be saved. All the children of Yemen are Amal.

Dr. Taha Al-Washalli, PhD Research Fellow in Water Supply Engineering at the UNESCO-IHE Institute for Water Education, spoke about the impact of the war on the water sector. Fourteen and one-half million of the 27.8 million inhabitants of the "poorest, most populous, and youngest nation on the Arabian Peninsula" currently lack access to water and sanitation, 8.2 million acutely. Fourteen million eight hundred thousand lack health services. Seven million people urgently need food. Two million two hundred thousand people have fled or lost their homes, and are internally displaced. Unemployment is at 52% (up from 37% before the war). Eighty-five percent of the population lives below the poverty line (up from 54% before the war).

According to UN figures, as of November 2016 at least 10,000 people have been killed, 60% by airstrikes; 75 are killed or injured every day. Almost thirteen thousand people have been hit by a cholera outbreak as a result of the collapse of water services. Quoting recent research by Martha Mandy, UK, Dr. Al-Washali said that "data from several sources strongly suggests that the Saudi Yemen Campaign contains a program for the destruction of rural livelihoods. Only 2.8% of Yemen's land is cultivated. To hit this small amount of agricultural land, you have to target it."

There were "357 bombings targeting farms, food stores, food trucks, etc.," Dr. Al-Washali continued. Already before the war, 90% of the wheat and 100% of the rice had to be imported. Under the ongoing blockade, people are being hit with massive price increases, while salaries have been massively cut since September 2015. He concluded that the damage inflicted on Yemen is wide, extended, long-term and hard to recover from. All of the major cites are affected.

The next speaker, Engeline Kramer, a specialist in intercultural communication and conflict resolution, stressed the hospitality, kindness and warmth of the

Cofounder of Mona Relief, Dr. R.S. Karim, addressing the Berlin conference on Yemen.

Yemeni people. She then asked "what is actually left in Yemen to destroy?" War criminals like George W. Bush, Jr., and Tony Blair must be brought to The Hague and face trial. The U.S.A., Great Britain and Germany could end the economic boycott immediately. Peace in Yemen must be supported, she demanded, quoting a saying: "Many small people who in many small places do many small things can alter the face of the world."

Dr. R.S. Karim, co-founder of Mona Relief-Yemen Organization for Humanitarian Relief and Development, spoke next. Mona is one of the few charity organizations on the ground in Yemen. "Yemen is a scarred country, an open wound, a shadow of its own former self," he said. "Saudi officials have closed Yemen to the world. They have locked the country. This is genocide." With 90% of food imported before the war, how do you feed 90% of the population with the remaining 10% of food? Every time a child dies from starvation it has been killed by someone.

He spoke to the horrified audience about women delivering stillborn babies who have died from hunger. He spoke of fathers contemplating suicide in despair be-

A girl pushing two children and water containers in a wheelbarrow in Yemen.

was presented, as was the beautiful perspective for Yemen in a New Paradigm of "Win-Win" cooperation.

Links Provided by Ulf Sandmark

Here are the two most important links that document the genocide against Yemen:

Yemen's Legal Center for Rights and Development: http://lcrdye. org/Eng/Default.aspx

International Yemen activists on facebook: https://www.facebook. com/StopTheWarOnYemen/

Among media you have: Al Masdar news in English: https:// mobile.almasdarnews.com/article/ category/yemen/

cause they cannot protect their families. "This misery stains the soul."

"Yemen is a humanitarian black hole. The country's dignity has been taken away." But above all, "Yemenis smell the stench of betrayal." Dr. Karim concluded: "When a military power deliberately targets children, there is only one thing you can do: Fight. Every father will fight. Every mother will become a tigress. Let's not allow Yemen to become another forgotten crisis. The war in Yemen is not the forgotten war of the decade, it is the shame of our generation!"

Lastly, Hassna, a young student, spoke about war crimes and the suffering of women and children, with many pictures echoing all the horrors that had been presented to the participants. After a concluding statement in Arabic, another recitation from the Quran and the playing of the Yemeni national anthem closed the conference.

The silence about the atrocities being committed in Yemen that was brought up many times during this conference was only underlined by the utterly shameful fact that apart from *EIR*, there were no representatives of the press or other media present, even though the conference took place in the very building of a prominent left-leaning newspaper.

Yet, the conference was a powerful success, not only in demonstrating and justly condemning the horror being brought down upon the people and the country of Yemen. The will to resist this injustice was palpable. Importantly, the larger problem of the British Empire

Further Links

1. http://english.aawsat.com/2017/02/article/ 55366693/unicef-63000-yemeni-children-died- 2016-malnutrition
2. https://www.unicef.org/media/media_93868.html
3. http://www.un.org/press/en/2015/sc11859.doc.htm
4. http://www.oxfam.org.uk/media-centre/press- releases/2016/12/yemen-running-out-of-food
5. http://reliefweb.int/report/yemen/under-secretary- general-humanitarian-affairs-and-emergency-relief- coordinator-11
6. https://www.oxfam.org/en/pressroom/pressreleases/ 2016-08-14/closure-yemens-main-airport-puts- millions-people-risk
7. http://www.independent.co.uk/news/world/middle- east/ministry-of-defence-saudi-arabia-coalition- forces-yemen-clsuter-bombs-humanitarian-law- violations-a7549581.html
8. https://sputniknews.com/amp/politics/ 201505021021620895/
9. http://www.dawn.com/news/1174185
10. http://samaacenter.org/publications/item/68-yemen- at-the-un.html
11. http://www.europarl.europa.eu/news/en/news- room/20160223IPR15513/stop-shelling-civilians- in-yemen-urge-meps
12. https://www.aiib.org/en/projects/approved/2016/ oman-railway-system.html

V. Man's Access to Reality

On Composing a New Future

The following are edited transcripts from two sources. The first part is from a discussion which Lyndon La-Rouche conducted with members of the LaRouche PAC Science Team on Feb. 23, 2017, and the second part consists of edited remarks from the Feb. 23 LaRouche PAC National Activist Call,[1] delivered by John Sigerson, member of the Board of Directors of Schiller Institute, Inc., and National Music Director of Schiller Institute.

Jason Ross: What is it to be productive? People are so divorced from an idea of productivity, young people have no idea what productivity means. ... The general theme has got to be, "how do we increase productivity, what is productivity, what are the ways that that gets fostered both through Glass Steagall and National Banking, to make it possible for manufacturing to return—including the public works aspect of it—on the science front, the fusion front, and on the infrastructure platform front." The potential productivity of the whole nation takes a tremendous leap with a high speed rail network, the maglev rail network, and there is this problem that people have in thinking about this when they are looking at it piece by piece rather than the platform that is generated as the whole. So those are some of the things I want to change.

Lyndon LaRouche: Well, some of these things you might not want to change—if you think carefully, because these issues don't come in numbers. They aren't simple quantities. What they do is they represent an action of the mind of people and it is the action of the mind of people that determines what action is in reality. So, therefore, you don't go to a quantity directly. You have an effect, which looks like something otherwise. But what you have to do is, you have to get to the gut of the issue itself. Hmm? You can't, in other words, make different kinds of combinations or work them out. That doesn't work. If it's serious, you have to discover what the meaning of what you just saw, was. In other words,

1. The entire dialogue with John Sigerson may be found at: http:// action.larouchepac.com/national_call_february_23

you cannot go by deduction, simple deduction. You have to actually develop a conception of how the whole system might work, and then work down to discover what that system means.

It's the creation of the creation of an idea, which apparently came from nowhere, but was just suddenly there. Then you have to find out what that meant. You have to investigate what was the way in which this thing happened. You can't do it by anatomic dissection. Some will do that dissection, but.... I don't think we want to do that in the public streets.

Ben Deniston: Can you say more about what you mean when you say "discover how the system works as a whole?"

LaRouche: Yes, the idea is, you cannot make a deductive approach to accomplish any system. It has to be something which evolves with the independent character, distinct from other characters which have been experienced otherwise. Therefore, it has to be a justification for this characterization.

Real discovery—all real discovery—is not pragmatic. It's always creative. You create something, in action, which would not have happened otherwise. In other words, everything that fits in, that comes in by definition itself, and it does not come because it's a combination of things—it becomes a servant of an idea. But the servant of the idea is not something which was composed in a formal way. That's why the so-called practical approaches to scientific work become a disaster. Because you have to deal with something which you can make this something—you can change it without changing the character of the thing.

So you get something which is independent of the particular thing, because the particular thing is not the solution. But you've got to find something that is so important to what you are trying to do, that you'll stick to that and not drift off into another direction. And that characteristic, these same kinds of discoveries, are not discoveries which can be quantified. They can appear to be quantified, but they're not of that character. It's like

Statue of Johannes Kepler in the gardens of the castle at Linz.

CC/Aldaron

creating a solar system, or a stellar system. It is not something you make by composing it, as such. It's something that you have to call upon in order to create, to stimulate the creation of an idea which otherwise would not exist.

Ross: Composition without components.

LaRouche: That's right! But composition with composition. So there has to be a relationship between the composition and what could have been otherwise the component. It is like making babies! You can sit it there in the crib all the way through life. But this crib does not define the baby! I hope it does not. What you are looking for is something, an idea which is necessary for a purpose, that is not something you simply deduce. Deduction process is not the means of dealing with that.

Megan Beets: Rather than making babies, I was going to say it is like making music, because the notes are necessitated by the idea.

LaRouche: Would we hope that's the way it is going to work out. Like our friend we discussed a time ago ... the composer you liked in the particular way, we discussed it. Kepler. Because it's a completely different composition. It does not have compositions as such. It has something which has a higher order of composition as such. And that's how all good things generally come about. Furtwängler was the man who made a very important turn in the understanding of composition, musical composition. That's an example of what we mean in creativity. It's not something you can add in numerically or any other way like that. It is something that you have to feel and create. And nothing else will do. And Furtwängler's case is typical of that—in the latter years of his life when he came to the greatest degree of development of his powers.

That's the difference between what you can make—by making some kind of dough or something—and creating a new idea which had no anticipation as such. Somebody did, somebody saw the idea, but they didn't make the idea. They adapted themselves to the idea, because it is something they understood, something they had understood, only lately. That's how great ideas come about. Like Furtwängler. Furtwängler was a very important figure in my life time.

Everything that is really good is of that same nature, is composed not by putting parts together... The important thing is what is necessary to create a new reality in the world, as Furtwängler did. Just take the closing end of Furtwängler's famous composition. That's what makes the music. Not the parts. So that's what I think our problem is, is to get a conception which is inherently intrinsic, and when the composer or the person who is functioning as if he were a composer, and effectively so, that you get a special kind of reaction in the composition as such. And that's what I think is in real scientific work—the location of the scientific principle, just like a musical principle, like Furtwängler, and put that together. Now you have something which comes *alive*; alive in its own way, its own characteristics. Anybody can make a poem but very few people are competent to develop compositions. So you want to have compositions—an inherently, intrinsic characteristic of something which is composed. And the ability that this thing represents for a productive achievement—that is what the point is you have to shoot for.

That is what Krafft Ehricke did. If you look at what Krafft Ehricke did in the United States, for example, it was unique. The way he died reminded us, those of us who knew him—realized that this was a composition made by a human being, Krafft Ehricke. And the whole thing was something unique, and you would turn around and say, well, "Krafft Ehricke—What does Krafft Ehricke mean?" Krafft Ehricke means the creative powers of a person, a highly developed person, who elevated mankind to a higher level of development.

So the fact that this idea of composition was situated in those terms is exactly what you have to do if you want to do what we are doing here. You can't synthesize something. You have to actually create it. And the creation is based on something which is *inside* what you are doing, but you could *never* interpret it. It could interpret you, but you cannot interpret it. This is the best way to get something worthwhile. Concentrate on that objective. If you want to cook something, always cook a composition. A composition is cooked, it is not made... I mean what are we doing here? We are taking a phenomenon, it is really strange, it is a phenomenon!

Société Wilhelm Furtwängler/furtwangler.net

Wilhelm Furtwängler conducting in Italy in 1949.

That's why it is there—it's a phenomenon. It is not a fact—it's a phenomenon, in the same way that Furtwängler set up his programs. So you want to create something that in and of itself has power, the power of creativity. And you will never get a simple answer. That would be wrong. If you did the right thing, then you would create something. But you wouldn't make it out of parts. Musical composition, the same thing. And it's fun. That's the other part. If it's not fun, don't do it!

Deniston: One aspect of this is what you went after very early on, the whole information theory fraud. You have often said that was a major part of your economic work, the fallacy of information theory as a methodological approach to any kind of system, like an economy. It seems like it has also permeated science and fundamental physics, to a degree I didn't even realize. It seems like information theory—literally breaking down the universe into a digitalized fundamental framework of yes/no information—appears to be actually a fundamental tenet of modern physics. It seems like that's another angle on the permeation of this completely fallacious methodological, epistemological view, not just in the economics as you cited then, but in science more generally.

LaRouche: It is not the action. It is the effect. And it is the effect you create—it's what makes the meaning of a text ... what makes it work. It does not work by composition as such. It functions itself by being able to repeat or to develop something out of an idea, but an idea which is in itself creative. And that's the formulation which is crucial. And people fail because they try to make things up. It's when they realize that something has come over them, it has an intrinsic value. It has no literal composition; it just has itself and that's what makes history great.

Like Furtwängler. He had an innovation, a capacity for innovation in a certain part of his life and that's the way it worked. And if you listen to Furtwängler's performances in life, that's what you see, that's what you get. There is no piece. There is a composition, a composition in a very special meaning—that you have an idea and this idea which flows from you on the basis of your discovery, is something unique, and is precious to you, it's precious to mankind. That's like the Furtwängler composition, his... composition, in the leading edges of what he did.

But Furtwängler's practice, and what he said about things, and what he did in response to this idea, is clear. It can be accessed. So the idea that music, composition, that the same thing is applied to all kinds of important things which are composition. When something comes out of your mind and suddenly says something that mind has never spoken before—and yet on a second thought, the person who is expressing that thing will respond to what he or she had intended. The meaning of that experience suddenly becomes something—a force more powerful than any mere idea. And that's what mankind has to achieve, the necessity is to get mankind to grasp *this idea*. Where do great ideas come from, what are great ideas, what do they represent? And that's the secret of science.

The same thing is discovering what Krafft Ehricke did in his work. He created things, new things, entirely new things coherent with the coherent systematic quality. Out of this thing, a whole story begins to evolve as something which has never been seen before. The point is to get rid of the amateurs. The amateurs are no use to science. When all the stars you want to study represent mankind as a whole, that's what you have to do. The problem is that most of the great politicians have no intellect. They only have bad. But the Furtwängler case is really a very good example of what the issue is. It is the idea of how do you create something which is beautiful. What is beauty? There is no such thing as beauty in the simple sense. It's the effect. Beauty lies in the effect it represents. I think by now you probably see more clearly what my argument is. And for me that's the principle of composition. It has many aspects and expressions but they all have one quality.

The National Activist Call

John Sigerson: Hello everybody. I wanted to approach what we're doing from a standpoint which I hope will make you happy. What we're doing is not just protecting the presidency; we're actually "composing" the presidency—that's our job. When I say "composing," I mean composing from the standpoint of, say, a poetic composition. Just today, Lyndon LaRouche was having a discussion with some of our people and he pointed out along these lines, and I quote, "Anyone can make a poem, but very few people can make a real composition, that is, a composition that has an underlying

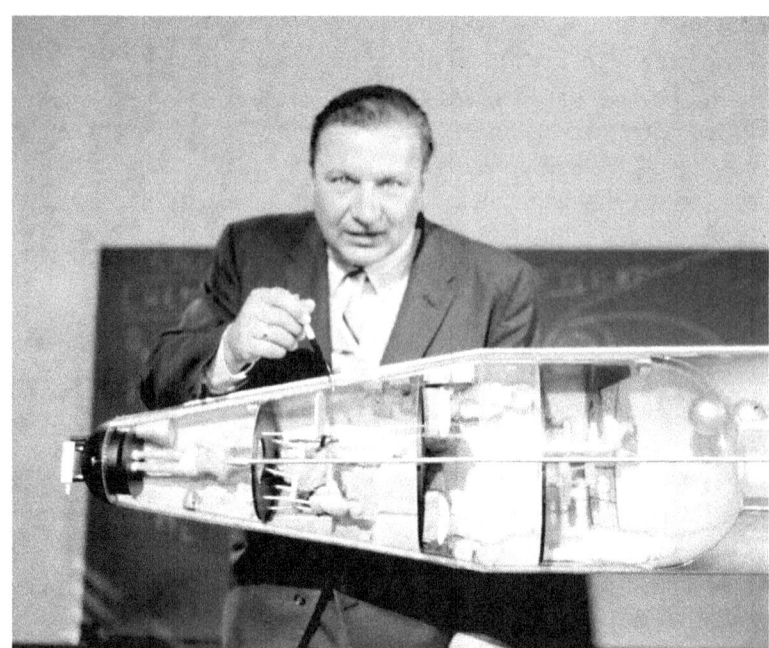

San Diego Air and Space Museum Archives

Krafft Ehricke, with model of a four-person Atlas Manned Space Station.

idea, a principle behind it." And this began to strike me with the Trump Presidency the other day, when he gave his very combative press conference to the media, attacking the media, which I'm sure you heard about, and probably listened to. At last Saturday's Manhattan Meeting, I pointed out something which struck me, which is the way he used the term "the *failing New York Times.*" And I sensed a note of poetry in what the President was doing there, because he said it a number of times, and it created a kind of breath of fresh air for me, and I think for everybody, because it broke a taboo, which is you're never supposed to say anything bad about the *New York Times.* It changed the whole attitude of the population, without people even knowing about it. We've seen the results of that even in our organizing over the last week, and I'm sure we're going to hear reports about that.

There was another incident with the President that I wanted to point out, which is even more amazing, which was the—you may have heard about this—the comments that Trump made in commemorating Black History Month. He was talking about Frederick Douglass, who of course was an incredible fighter in the 19th Century against slavery. President Trump said the following, "Frederick Douglass is an example of someone who has done an amazing job and is getting recognized more and more, I notice."

The liberal media went absolutely wild over what

Trump said. Why? You would say, well, why is that? Let me read you what the *Washington Post* said. "The world may never know whether President Trump just got a little sloppy with his verb tenses on Wednesday morning, or simply had no idea that the famous black abolitionist Frederick Douglass was in fact dead." In other words, what they are quibbling over is the fact that he used the verb "is" rather than "was."

This is exactly the kind of violation of rules which is the core of anything having to do with poetry. There is a book called the *New York Times Manual of Style* and there is also a similar book by Strunk and White called *Elements of Style* which may have been inflicted on many of you in your studies, which outline all the rules you are supposed to follow in order to communicate something, and all of these rules are, especially with commas—you're not supposed to use a comma except grammatically in order to throw off certain kinds of phrases. And you're not supposed to use "is" if you're talking about something in the past—and all of these kinds of crazy rules. Obviously, what President Trump was saying—and that's what his press spokesman said later on—that obviously Trump was thinking of Frederick Douglass' legacy as being completely alive and growing, which I think is a wonderful idea. What's the problem with that?

That brings me to this question of poetry, and I think that we all have to be thinking, as we're doing all of the things that we're doing—we have to be thinking that ultimately it is poetry, a certain kind of poetry—polemical poetry—that actually changes the entire paradigm of the population.

I just wanted to read something from Percy Shelley. It's his essay, *A Defense of Poetry*. If you've ever read this essay, it's not that long but it's incredibly packed, and you may have heard bits and pieces of it. I just wanted to read one passage here, where he says:

Painting by Alfred Clint

Percy Bysshe Shelley

At such periods—and I would say such periods as the one that we're living through *right now*[John Sigerson]—there is an accumulation of the power of communicating and receiving intense and impassioned conceptions respecting man and nature. The persons in whom this power resides, may often, as far as regards many portions of their nature, have little apparent correspondence with that spirit of good of which they are the ministers, but even while they deny and abjure, they are yet compelled to serve, the power which is seated on the throne of their own soul. It is impossible to read the compositions of the most celebrated writers of the present day without being startled with the electric life which burns within their words

Okay. Let me read that according to the way that the *New York Times Manual of Style* would read it. [Reads it again as described.] I guess you can get the idea that also it is very important that things are presented in an emphatic way; and the key there of course is that I eliminated all the commas, which is exactly what is usually done nowadays. And that is what the liberals like. They don't like commas, at all.

What is this thing called poetry? I just want to read a little bit more from earlier on, where Shelley says something about what poetry is. He says:

Poetry, in a general sense, may be defined to be the expression of the imagination: and poetry is connate with the origin of man. Man is an instrument over which a series of external and internal impressions are driven, like the alternations of an ever-changing wind over an Æolian lyre, [that's a musical instrument], which move it by their motion to ever-changing melody. But there is a principle within the human being, and perhaps within all sentient beings, which acts otherwise than in the lyre, and produces not melody alone, but harmony, by an internal adjustment of the sounds or motions thus excited to the impressions which excite them. It is as if the lyre could accommodate its chords to the motions of that which strikes them, in a determined proportion of sound; even as the musician can accommodate his voice to the sound of the lyre. [And skipping a little bit, he talks about the child's delight in these things, and he says,] In relation to the objects which delight a child, these expressions are what poetry is to higher objects.

And indeed, what we are talking about is that higher object.

Over the recent period, we've been re-issuing a number of wonderful written pieces by Lyndon LaRouche, which if you have not worked on, you really should work through. I would just point out that there are a couple of pieces that are very, very critical, which you could listen to or study in order to get a sense of that. These are pieces which I'll probably be working on, giving a class series, as well. One of them is a piece by Mozart, which is called *Ave Verum Corpus*. It's a seemingly very simple piece. It means "Hail True Body." It's a song to the Virgin Mary, but it has embedded in it this exact same principle that I'm getting at here, and it also points to an incredible piece that was later written by Beethoven which is a string quartet, which is *Opus 132*, which has in it something that harkens back to Mozart, whom of course Beethoven revered. It's "a holy song of thanks to the Godhead of one who has been cured," and that is also something very beautiful.

The other thing that I would like (again, just for time, we can't really work these things through here, but I will) is to work through something that has preoccupied me for many years, and ought to preoccupy everyone, which is the work of the great conductor Wilhelm Furtwängler, who was a German conductor and German music director; and who, if you want to understand what really is motivating Lyndon LaRouche—and I say "is" and will continue to motivate Lyndon LaRouche—you must work through the effect that Furtwängler's work, and the pieces that he conducted had on LaRouche, as he was growing up. I will just point out that there was one point, in 1946, when Lyndon LaRouche was in India and he heard for the first time a recording—which I actually dug up—it's a 1938 recording by Furtwängler, doing a piece by Tchai-

kovsky, the Russian composer; and in a footnote, in another work which we will probably be publishing, called "Man's Original Creations,"[2] which he wrote in 2005, that is, at the age of 83, he said:

As I have often, on occasion, referred to this experience, the first time I experienced Furtwängler's conducting was in 1946, in hearing a recording of his directing of a Tchaikovsky performance. It was like a 'Damascus Road' experience, in which I recognized that the effect I experienced, of the 'transparency' of the performance, lay in a gripping cross-voice movement throughout the performance, to the effect of the relentlessness of a compelling sense of a seamless intellectual development underlying the heard music which is heard not with the ear, but with the mind.

And it is precisely that musical sense which if we are able to get that across and communicate this in everything that we do, we will win. With that, I will hand it over to questions and answers.

In response to a question concerning the political organizing in New York City, John said the following:

Sigerson: OK. Well, A___, I just have to keep hammering away at this question of *irony*. This wonderful article that Lyn wrote called "Man's Original Creations" which we quoted before, talks about this thing, because that's the way to put it into words. Let me just read the paragraph that Lyn wrote:

As Schiller emphasizes, the man from the street should leave the theater as virtually a different person than had entered a few hours before. *Irony!* This effect is not, like the experience of some fundamentalist parson's rant, some maudlin sort of edifying moral effect upon the audience. It is the effect on the citizen of looking over the shoulder of a history different than that of his own experience of life in his own time and place. [We're talking about great drama, like Shakespeare now.] *Irony!* "Why could they not see the rottenness of their culture? Could I do something about a tragic error in the culture of my own society today? What kind of a fool I would be, if I could not look at my own culture

---

2. See the article on page XX, in this issue of *EIR*

as I could now see so clearly the insanity of that other culture presented to me by that play?" *Irony!* He is not such a fool that he would attempt to deduce a principle for his culture from the other culture on stage.

But then later on, a wonderful paragraph that I really love, Lyn says,

The orbit of the planets is not circular, but elliptical. *Irony!* Fermat demonstrated that the pathway of least action is not the shortest distance, but the pathway of the quickest time. *Irony!* Huyghens thought this pathway was defined by the cycloid; but Leibniz and Bernoulli demonstrated that it is the catenary-defined principle of the Leibniz calculus, the principle of universal least action. *Irony!*

And indeed, the more ironical juxtapositions that you're able to do, when you're even talking to people, it requires a little bit more concentration, a little bit more effort, but that's why I brought up this irony—earlier on here—about this crazy thing with Frederick Douglass, because it points out the ironical juxtaposition of *how crazy* all the media are at this point, so that people can actually laugh at it—as Trump was laughing at it.

The Activist Call concluded with these final comments:

Sigerson: I want to add one thing to what Dennis just said, on a political note, which is something that Lyndon LaRouche was very emphatic about earlier on, this week, which is *Obama personally.* Lyndon said very explicitly, "We have to destroy Obama." That doesn't mean physically, but right now we have an opportunity to destroy his credibility, destroy everything that he represents. And Lyndon was very explicit on saying that we should focus also on the Tuesday kill sessions, that Obama was doing: He is a murderer. He continues to be a murderer, and everything that he's doing right now is pushing towards murder even of the sitting President of the United States. And I think that we should *not be nice to Obama.* We should really pile it on with this guy, because he should get everything that he deserves. He should be discredited and *a good part of the population now may actually be able to take*

that Damascus Road. People who up to now have been sort of dumb supporters.

And I think some of these meetings, especially the one that P__ just mentioned, is a perfect example of that kind of thing. They're ripe for conversion, and almost like, I would say, "deprogramming."

Otherwise, I just want to urge people not to ignore these incredible works that now we're re-issuing in *Executive Intelligence Review,* on these incredibly, for some of you, possibly quite difficult to read, longer pieces by Lyndon. Because if you want sticking power, which is what this movement has had for now almost 50 years, if you want sticking power, you've got to learn to know Mr. LaRouche in the deepest way possible. He's still around, he's 94 years old now, and you can still talk to him, but it's these papers that really reveal as deeply as you're going to get, his soul. And really, avail yourself of this opportunity; Mr. LaRouche is one of the greatest thinkers of the past millennium and a lot of us, reading these papers, and re-reading these papers myself, have reinforced that idea. It's not an exaggeration: future generations will, I think, bear this out. Thank you.

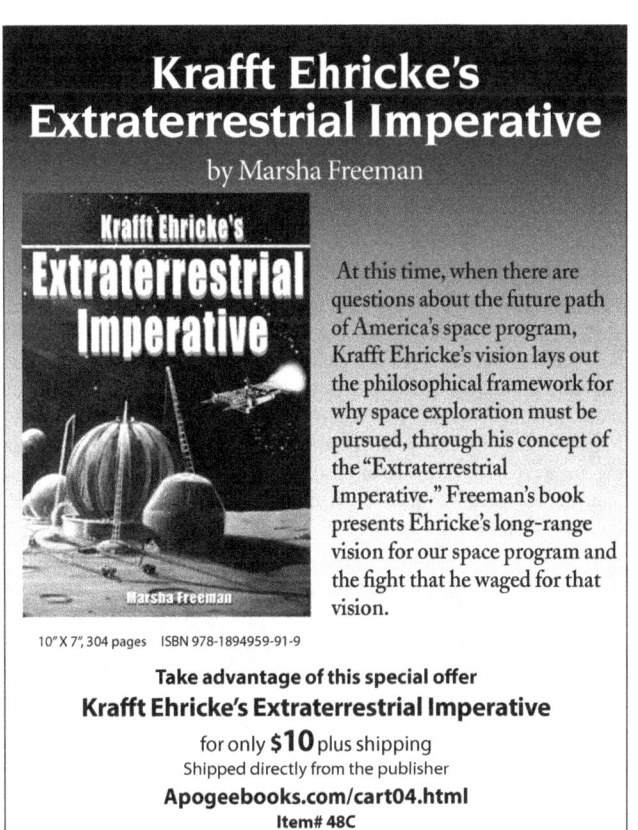

DISCUSSION ON SCIENCE WITH HELGA

Man's Original Creations

by Lyndon H. LaRouche, Jr.

June 6, 2005

Foreword

Recently, my wife, Helga Zepp-LaRouche, reminded me, that Cardinal Nicholas of Cusa had emphasized that man's discovery of universal physical principles changed the universe in the sense of generating newly created agencies. It should be noted that Helga's continuing studies of the work of Cusa, which have been continued, with varying intensity, during approximately three decades, were begun during the mid-1970s, and were begun, with my emphatic encouragement, in frequent consultation with Professor Haubst of the Cusanus Gesellschaft, then the world's leading expert on Cusa.[1]

In our inner-family dialogue on this matter, we were

---

1. Cusa had founded a home for retired clergy in his native town whose name he bears, Bernkastel-Kues, athwart the Mosel where his father had fished for crabs. For related reasons, I have often visited Cusa's still-operating foundation in Helga's company, including a well-attended 1987 celebration, on the occasion of my 65th birthday, where my now recently deceased friend, the leader of the famous Amadeus Quartet, Norbert Brainin, performed in my honor. Cusa's chapel and library are maintained up to last report, and the foundation is supported, at least in part, by the proceeds of the annual sales of its wine. Cusa is outstanding for several special accomplishments which have been proven by later developments to have been essential to the founding of modern civilization: his design for the founding of the modern sovereign nation-state (**Concordantia Catholica**), ending the Venetian-Norman tyranny of the *ultramontane* system; his founding of the modern experimental physical science of Luca Pacioli, Leonardo da Vinci, and of such among Kepler's followers as Fermat and Leibniz, and Leibniz's followers such as Carnot, Arago, Ampère, Gauss, Wilhelm Weber, Dirichlet, and Riemann (**De Docta Ignorantia**); his crucial contribution to the success of the great ecumenical Council of Florence; and, his founding of the project which inspired Christopher Columbus's voyage of trans-Atlantic discovery. Professor Haubst's own work on the legacy of Cusa has left a living record of inspired and energetic devotion and scholarly excellence.

both right. She was correct, on her representation of Cusa's argument, and I on mine. The explanation of that seemingly paradoxical point will be currently of interest among relevant members of the international LaRouche Youth Movement (LYM) and also others; therefore, I supply the relevant explanation of the point as follows.

As I emphasize in the following pages, there are two aspects to any validatable discovery of a universal principle of the physical universe. This includes, as efficiently physical principles, those true principles of Classical artistic composition on which our association has worked over past decades, including the role of C=256 cycles in Well-Tempered, Florentine *bel canto* modes of musical composition and its performance. The first aspect of all validatable discovery of universal principles, is the way in which the mind of the relevant human individual discovers a pre-existing universal principle *in its expression as a potential*; but, then, second, we require an experimentally valid proof of that same potential, which, when discovered and also practiced by man, then serves mankind in a way which changes the universe, a new discovery of some principle which, at least implicitly, increases mankind's power in, and over the universe. Cusa's work embraced both aspects of this process of discovery, but, as Helga correctly emphasized, Cusa emphasizes the second, man in his role as a creator in the sacred likeness of the Creator. Cusa did this in a way which defines him in retrospect today, as the most significant of those Renaissance thinkers who defined the broad conceptions on which the specific achievements of modern European civilization, relative to earlier times, were premised.

Thus, the originality of mankind's original discovery of a principle, lies in the act of discovery of a universal implication of the existing universe, a *potentiality* which had been previously hidden from the view of mankind's knowledge. Man's acting on the basis of that discovered *potentiality*, changes the universe, bringing it into a new dynamic state. This, once again, confirms Heracleitus' and Plato's view, that in the universe, there is no exception to the continuation of qualitative change as the underlying ontological reality of processes.[2] The universe is not a domain within which changes in principle are sometimes permitted; the universe is always being changed in this way, changing itself in this way, as Heracleitus and Plato, for example, insisted, and as V.I. Vernadsky insisted, in his development of the concepts of Biosphere and Noösphere.

Markus Norman

Lyndon LaRouche and Helga Zepp-LaRouche. "In our inner-family dialogue on this matter, we were both right," writes Mr. LaRouche, respecting their discussion of the importance of the contributions of Cardinal Nicholas of Cusa.

Thus, Helga and I were both right.

This should bring the attention of all among us present on this occasion, to the subject of the term "realization": to the subject of the way in which we should employ that term in scientific practice. That includes, of course, the subject in which I have accumulated original and otherwise notable qualities of expertise, the subject of an applied science of physical economy, as first defined by Gottfried Leibniz during his relevant work of the interval 1671-1716.

Since the circulation of my recent "Vernadsky and Dirichlet's Principle" featured in the June 3 edition of the ***Executive Intelligence Review*** news weekly,[3] there has been accelerated attention to the subject of "dynamics" among my associates, especially the LaRouche Youth Movement. Notably, my associates Bruce Director, Dr. Jonathan Tennenbaum, and relevant members of the LYM, among others, have accelerated their educational work on the subject of physical science, as modern teaching in economics and

other relevant specialities must be redefined for current and future practice of humanity generally, defined from the standpoint of Riemann's Theory of Abelian Functions.

It is to be emphasized here, that throughout this report as a whole, the term "power" as employed in the following pages, is the English translation of the German term *Kraft*, as used by Leibniz in both his founding of the science of physical economy, and in his redefining the basis for all physical science after the work of Cusa's follower Kepler. It should be remembered, in reading the following report, that Leibniz's use of this notion of power is expressed in those notions of *dynamics* expressed by Leibniz's discovery and development, in association with Jean Bernouilli, of the only competent basis for a calculus, the catenary-based principle of universal physical least action. Otherwise, all of my successes, as contrasted with the failures, heretofore, of most of my professional rivals in the field of economic forecasting, have depended upon rejecting the mechanistic method relied upon in the visible arguments which had been previously presented by my putative rivals.

Lately, as the presently onrushing economic collapse of the world's present monetary-financial system reaches

---

2. The modern form of this view of the argument of the permanence of qualitative change in principle, as by Heracleitus and Plato, is expressed in modern physical science by Bernhard Riemann's 1857 presentation of the theory of Abelian Functions.

3. *Executive Intelligence Review*, June 3, 2005.

EIRNS/Ulla Cicconi

Nicolas of Cusa (1401-1464) was born here in Bernkastel-Kues; inset, a replica of Cusa's tomb. "Cusa is outstanding for several special accomplishments which have been proven by later developments to have been essential to the founding of modern civilization...."

its climax, my richly vindicated, long-standing views on the subject of economy have been favorably reassessed by many who, in earlier times, had wished to consider my warnings as somewhat exaggerating the dangers, if not simply wrong. Thus, at a time when many in the U.S.A. and elsewhere are inclined to accept my assessments and proposals as important, they tend, nonetheless, to worry all the more; they fear, that in their accepting what they now tend to admire in my work, they might tend to overlook my possible errors on related other accounts. I am therefore obliged to attempt, once again, to make the entirety of my methods and world-outlook transparent to those increased numbers of influentials and others who consider it important to know the fuller implications of my outlook, beyond what is expressed as explicitly on the subject of economy.

My referenced recent, brief discussion with Helga on the subject of Cusa's work, is therefore an appropriate starting-point for addressing such a wider range of matters.

Although I can trace the source of my discoveries in the field of physical economy to what I have often re-

ported, earlier, as an incident at the beginning of my attendance in a secondary-school geometry semester,[4] I have not yet decided, nearly seventy years later, how much this incident prompted my adoption of Leibniz's influence, and how much my already ravenous appetite for English renderings of French, English, and German philosophers of the Seventeenth and Eighteenth centuries had contributed to that statement which I had made during the course of the first hour of that semester's geometry class. What is certain is that, from about that time, I was, and have remained a persuaded follower of Leibniz.

What has been technically wrong with the work, and opinions of my notable rivals in the field of economic analysis and forecasting, is just that. They had taken the wrong turn at the crossroads in their choice of method. As a result of their induced preference for the methods of Paolo Sarpi's empiricism, in opposition to those of Leibniz and his predecessors back as far as the Pythagoreans and Plato, these economists' previous failures have been rooted in their preference for mechanistic methods. The result was their earlier refusal to take into account those aspects of the actual nature of mankind on which competent long-term assessments in economy depend.

These economists, so far, had previously overlooked the relevance of the view of human nature shared by Leibniz, for defining all subject-matters of scientific and artistic significance in determining the effects called "economic." Vernadsky's combined conception of Biosphere and Noösphere, when considered as an outgrowth of the heritage of Leibniz, is the most appropriate choice of context for defining the application of an

---

4. See Lyndon H. LaRouche, Jr., "Science, The Power To Prosper," **EIR**, April 29, 2005, p. 6: "Some Relevant Personal Background."

economics as I have redefined the notion of a science of physical economy for the immediate future of mankind today. Therefore, on this occasion, I turn attention here to the broader cultural implications of Vernadsky's dynamic conception of the universe and society.

1. Economy As Art and Physical Science

The most obvious indication of the existence of a higher class of fossils, those which are produced by means other than ordinary kinds of living processes, is the working archeologist's discovery of residues which could not have come into being by any means other than the agency of a specifically human intelligence. Such residues, belonging to V.I. Vernadsky's *Noösphere*, are to be defined as products of the application of a universal physical principle which existed *implicitly,* in the form of a *potential*, prior to mankind's employment of it, but which did not exist, as the residue of a practiced natural phenomenon, prior to mankind's discovery and application of the principles expressed by those archeological or comparable residues. The power efficiently expressed by intention, as evident in the successful employment of such principles, is a potentiality which may be expressed in the form of a residue of social action, but is to be regarded, more emphatically, as a residue of a principle which has come into existence as a practicable idea only within the sovereign bounds of the individual human mind which has discovered it.

All competent practice of archeology as a branch of the work of the historian, hangs implicitly on that rigorous set of distinctions.

Hence, all competent accounts of history, as *the science of the history of the human species*, are based on the broader application of that same, more rigorous definition of the essential principle of archeology, as I have already restated this point within my recent *Vernadsky and Dirichlet's Principle*. Actual knowledge of history, including archeology as a branch of a science of history, is, essentially, *the history of ideas*: the history of those ideas which express the specific quality of mental activity leading to the discovery, or re-discovery of either a universal physical principle, or its Classical-artistic form of equivalent. These ideas are communicable only through the act of replication of a relevant original act of discovery by the sovereign cognitive processes of an individual human mind. These ideas generated by sovereign individual minds, are expressed in a communicable form, only through a special kind of tangible practice, practice of the type associated with the human, cognitive replication of an individual mind's experimentally validatable act of discovery of a universal physical principle.

In globally extended European cultures today, there is a more or less grudging acknowledgment by modern society, of the need to apply the term "universal principle" to relevant matters in the domain of what is termed "physical science"; but, the suggestion that the same notion might be applied to the domain of art, often provokes an unpleasant facial expression, still today. Therefore, let us begin with the role of a universal physical principle in Classical artistic composition.

The Case for Music

For an illustration of this point about artistic composition, choose, first, a certain, short composition of W.A. Mozart which is suitable for treatment by a relatively small chorus, *Ave Verum Corpus*. It is experimentally demonstrable, that this composition could not be competently performed according to Mozart's intention simply by a formally literate, schoolbook reading of the score by the director and members of the performing ensemble. The performance requires a form of instruction which lies in something above what some might consider the formal aspects of the score, something which lies in the interaction, across, or, if you prefer, "behind" the singing voices, in the progression of the performance as a whole. "This something" is, in this case of Mozart's piece, expressed through the role of the same Lydian mode treated famously by Beethoven's Opus 132 string quartet.[5]

The distinction in quality of performance to which I am referring here, is not an effect which the relevant composer did not intend. It was precisely his intention, as a series of examples from choral and instrumental music of leading Classical composers, most notably from Bach through Brahms, demonstrates that to be the case in principle. The musical score reflects the existence of a composer's intended potential for that composition, which the performers must bring to actuality.

---

5. See Mindy Z. Pechenuk, "Mozart's Ave Verum Corpus," **Fidelio**, Winter 1996. Mrs. Pechenuk directed a pedagogical performance at a Schiller Institute Conference, where the argument of her report was demonstrated in a live performance which is preserved in an audio-visual record retained to the present today.

EIRNS/Philip Ulanowsky

The Schiller Institute chorus, directed by John Sigerson, performs Mozart's "Ave Verum Corpus" on Aug. 31, 1996. Inset: Mindy Pechenuk leads a pedagogical discussion of Mozart's discoveries. To bring out Mozart's intention, the singers must pay attention to what lies "between the notes" of the score.

Although the tools of this Classical principle are traceable by us as far back as the Pythagoreans, and to the basis for this intention expressed by the surviving fragments of Leonardo da Vinci's **De Musica**, it is J.S. Bach who created the system of well-tempered counterpoint on which all of the leading Classical composers have depended.

The systemic quality of error which the performers of such music must combat in themselves, is that created by even professional musicians and others who, demonstrably, like the notorious cases of Rameau, Fux, and their admirers, lack comprehension of the species-nature of any relevant Classical composer's intention.[6]

The same species of challenge represented in the Mozart *Ave Verum Corpus*, is presented, for a second example, by an earlier choral work, the motet **Jesu, meine Freude** of J.S. Bach, which presents the choral director and chorus with the same principled kind of challenge represented by Mozart's *Ave Verum Corpus*.[7]

For example, that challenge, in both of these instances, has been addressed and demonstrated by John Sigerson's direction of the LaRouche Youth Movement's rehearsals and performances of that Bach work.[8] The selection of that Bach work for this purpose, was suggested by me, but endorsed by music director John Sigerson as a keystone for the East Coast development of the kind of LaRouche Youth Movement which had been developed earlier on the West Coast. This use of that Bach motet has been since continued on the West Coast, in Europe, and elsewhere. The progress of the choruses engaged in this project has been a rich lode of their expanding insights into the deeper implications of Bach's intention in this case, and a consequently growing insight into the intention of his life's work taken as a whole. Patient review of the relevant evidence available, shows that all the principal work of all leading Classical-musical composers, from J.S. Bach through

6. Rameau and Fux are a product of the modern reductionist corruption associated with the legacies of Paolo Sarpi and Descartes. They are, in that respect, authentic forerunners of the Romantic opponents of Bach's method, including the Carl Czerny whom Beethoven described as "that criminal" who would ruin Czerny's talented young pupil Franz Liszt. This is also a fault of Modernists and Post-Modernists, the latter including the school of Theodor Adorno's Brecht-like perversions.

7. The attempt to separate Bach from Haydn, Mozart, and Beethoven, on the alleged distinction between Baroque and Classical, or the like, is worse than merely useless gossip whose influence is too often expressed in performances by musicians affected by such chatter.

8. This is the same John Sigerson who organized and directed the project of our quite credible, mid-1980s performances of Mozart's Requiem, and who has played a leading, and progressive professional role in the vocal and other musical work of our association since then. The increasing refinement of his direction of the work with the youth and other choruses during the passage of time, is a reflection of the cumulative benefits of that continuing history.

Johannes Brahms, and great conductors, such as the late Wilhelm Furtwängler, are premised on the same attention to what "lies behind (or, "between") the notes" of the score.[9]

In providing students of music practical insight into the dynamic methods of Classical musical composition and performance, the way in which principle is expressed as a method of performance, is most readily referenced by pointing to how those examples may be managed by the skilled string quartet. Norbert Brainin described this to me, and also to relevant members of my circles of associates, as the method of rehearsal used by the members of the celebrated Amadeus Quartet, with results which can be heard from recordings by that institution. In the case of the Classical quartet, skilled performers can hear the relevant cross-voice intervals and adjust their performance in rehearsals according to the relevant dynamics of the composition. In the work of a chorus, or a larger instrumental ensemble, a director of the type which recorded examples of Wilhelm Furtwängler's directions illustrate, is implicitly required for this same purpose.[10]

Having each singer, or other performer come to a rehearsal with an "independent" reading of the notes in a part in the score, were often a recipe for standard qualities of artistic failures (unless the work being performed is itself already a modernist, post-modernist, or comparable abomination, whose message is a warning to the sensible member of the audience to leave the room). The relations among the individuals participating in musical performance of a Classical work in the Classical tradition of Bach through Brahms, for example, are not mechanical relations in the sense of the methods of the empiricists and other reductionists; they are *dynamic* in Leibniz's sense of that latter term of his

reproach against the incompetence of the reductionist René Descartes. They are *dynamic* in the sense of V.I. Vernadsky's argument respecting "organism," and my own argument, respecting principle, as I have presented and argued this point of both Vernadsky's and my own method in my already referenced ***Vernadsky and Dirichlet's Principle***.

The emergence of modalities, such as the referenced cases of the Lydian mode, as an ordering principle in the across-voice process of development of a composition's performance (as distinct from successions of vertical chords), is an example of Leibniz's notion of that *dynamic* principle as Vernadsky and I have defined it: as distinct from, and opposed to a mechanical connection. This time we situate it within the domain of Classical artistic composition, rather than only physical science. In art, this has the same quality of significance as a universal principle, as the rule of the ontologically existent infinitesimal in Leibniz's catenary-cued universal principle of physical least-action, the principle which Leibniz expressed by his original discovery of that concept of natural logarithmic functions, later imitated, in somewhat castrated form, by the actively Leibniz-hating Leonhard Euler.[11]

In musical performance, this principle is expressed in the relations among a polyphonic passage in the unfolding of the performance in local intervals, expressed by what the unwitting member of the audience might view as seemingly very slight deviations, which that member mistakenly regards as like a chef's Romantic personal touch of seasoning added to a standard recipe. To the witting, they are associated with a special kind of *tension* which lends a sense of movement associated with what is actually the deeper meaning of the term "development." As I shall explain below, this quality of *tension* in Classical polyphony in music is associated

---

9. The concept is congruent with Leibniz's definition of *Analysis Situs*, as this was carried forward in the work of Bernhard Riemann. It signifies the relevance of the ancient Pythagorean, *dynamic* notion of Leibniz's physical science and Bach's musical principles, as opposed to the formally *mechanistic* standpoint of Rameau, Fux, the Romantics, modernists, et al., and also the empiricists D'Alembert, Euler, Lagrange, et al.

10. As I have often, on occasion, referred to this experience, the first time I experienced Furtwängler's conducting was in 1946, in hearing a recording of his directing of a Tchaikovsky performance. It was like a "Damascus Road" experience, in which I recognized that the effect I experienced, of the "transparency" of the performance, lay in a gripping cross-voice movement throughout the performance, to the effect of the relentlessness of a compelling sense of a seamless intellectual development underlying the heard music which is heard not with the ear, but with the mind.

11. The principal targets of Carl F. Gauss's attack on the incompetence of the empiricists D'Alembert, Euler, Lagrange, et al., in Gauss's own 1799 doctoral dissertation on the subject of **The Fundamental Theorem of Algebra**, were each and all representations of a cult of Leibniz-haters which had been organized as a network of salons by a Paris-based Venetian, Descartes-admirer Abbé Antonio Conti (1677-1749). Since Conti believed that a French Descartes would not sell well in London of that time, Conti used a circle he organized in London to create a cult, directed by figures such as theologian Samuel Clarke, as controllers of the figure chosen to substitute for Descartes, the black-magic hobbyist Isaac Newton. Conti's network of salons, a network organized around Leibniz-hater Voltaire, became the vehicle of a Europe-wide cult of Isaac Newton, in which D'Alembert, Maupertuis, Euler, and Lagrange were leading figures.

The celebrated Amadeus Quartet in performance. Their genius lay in playing together "between the notes," bringing out the unity of the Classical composer's idea.

with those Classical expressions of *irony* which define the ironical principle of movement in poetry and Classical tragedy.

The controlling influence over this subtlety, as expressed in an acceptable performance of a Classical work, is unity of effect in the performance taken as an individual unit, a unity spreading, seamlessly, from a breath prior to the first tone, to a breath after the last. (There may appear to be "seams" in the literal structure of the score, *but not in the idea which must underlie the performance of that score*.) One knows that this intention has been chosen correctly as that of the composer, when the effect of the performance is that of a seamless and energetic unfolding of a valid choice of a single, unifying, underlying idea, "driving" the performance from beginning to close, producing this, a single idea, rather than a collection of musical effects. Beethoven's *opera* 131, 132, and 133, are recommendable testcases for showing this principle of composition and performance. Did the composition's performance "hang together?" "Did the composition as a whole move you, as by but a single, driving, truthful conception—in the sense of Riemann's representation of his relatively more advanced version of Dirichlet's Principle?"

It is of crucial importance that I emphasize here, that this conception is identical in all essentials with Riemann's notion of the application of what he references as Dirichlet's Principle, as I do in the case of my already referenced *Vernadsky and Dirichlet's Principle*.[12] One must hear the entire performance as a single, indivisible idea. This is accomplished by focussing on the relevant composer's intention to achieve a unity of effect in the process of development of the performance, such that the sensible performers and their audiences will hear the entire composition as a seamless garment, rather than a composite of separable parts of a mere mosaic, composed to produce the effect of a mere pattern, rather than an actual idea of principle.[13]

The genius specific of Beethoven's composition of such "late quartets" as his Opus 131, 132, and his *Grosse Fugue*, present a demonstration of that argument most clearly and emphatically; these are works of supreme genius precisely because they demonstrate the higher, dynamic principle of all Classical composition with such exquisitely intense purity of unity of effect. It is the same dynamic principle otherwise to be recognized as expressed by Leibniz's notion of his principle of universal physical least action, as an expression of what Riemann presented as his improved notion of what he termed "Dirichlet's Principle."

Clear ideas can not be distinguished as such without a rigorous regard for principle. On this account, the Classical chorus trained in Florentine *bel canto* tradition with register-shifts referenced to C=256, is necessary.[14] It is the slight adjustments in the quality of intonation needed to bring the focus upon the modalities expressed in forward motion, which are the singer's means for achieving the dynamic quality of unity of effect needed for a work such as the Mozart *Ave Verum Corpus*.

Consider the benefit such Classical musical compo-

12. The LaRouche Youth Movement has accepted the challenge of developing pedagogy which represents the Principle as Dirichlet presented it in the relevant lectures which his student Riemann attended in Berlin, and also as Riemann's corrected, higher conception of this in his own work on Abelian Functions later.

13. Wilhelm Furtwängler's recorded conducting of Franz Schubert's great C-Major Symphony, when compared with the work of his putative rivals of that time, provides an appropriate illustration of the point.

14. See *A Manual on the Rudiments of Tuning and Registration, Book I: Introduction and the Human Singing Voice*, John Sigerson, Kathy Wolfe, eds. (Washington, D.C.: Schiller Institute, 1992).

sitions and their appropriate performance represent for the working physical scientist. To bridge the apparent difference this implies, shift attention slightly to the principle expressed by those modes of both plastic and non-plastic artistic composition which are to be recognized as strictly Classical in both composition and in terms of the modes of performance applicable to such compositions. The same principle expressed by the referenced Beethoven quartets is to be found underlying the principle of composition and adequate performance of Classical poetry and tragedy.

Irony: The Classical Principle in Art

Today, the word "idea" is popularly employed in a manner which is, intrinsically, functionally illiterate. The strictly Classical use of that term, "idea," limits its use to conceptions of universal physical principle, or to Classical artistic conceptions produced in accord with that same standard of precise distinction. The prevalence of what is fairly termed "the factor of slop" in the prevailing standards of instruction and related practice, in both what is called physical science, especially in mathematics as such, and, worse, in defining principles of artistic composition, has had the effect of maintaining a state of affairs which has been usefully termed, as by Britain's late C.P. Snow, a "two cultures" crisis in modern European civilization, a separation of science from art. The fault lies on both sides of the professions; the results are grave in their impact on education; often, the moral effects of this condition has been catastrophic. Here, I employ the term "idea" in its proper, strictest sense of meaning as applying to both domains.

That idea of "slop" is typified by the method of D'Alembert's, Euler's, and Lagrange's attacks on Leibniz, as they were correctly attacked for such "slop" by Gauss's 1799 paper on the subject of the Fundamental Theorem of Algebra. They asserted simply algebraic methods in a "hand-waving" sort of brushing-aside of the fact of an essential ontological difference between a mere algebra and a subject in physical geometry, such as the ontological, geometrical difference among a point, line, surface, solid, etc. These empiricists, and others of kindred spirit, use a reductionist's notion of mechanics, as Euler and Lagrange did, as a substitute for actual scientific principle. In other words, they perpetrated a simple sort of intentional fraud, the same kind of fraud practiced by the followers of Rameau and Fux, relative to the work of Bach and his followers. Today, the same type of methodological fraud is pervasive, if, happily, not entirely so, in the domain of composition and performance of poetry and Classical drama.

Thus, the specific problem on which I ask you to focus your attention at this phase of the report, is the concept of Classical *irony,* as this is encountered as the essential principle of Classical poetry and drama. This kind of idea also appears as the concept of an efficient universal physical principle, and as this is expressed in the musical examples I have just referenced above.

Select four Shakespeare dramas chosen, on this occasion, for the purpose of illustrating that point: ***Julius Caesar***, and three dramatizations locating action within a legendary society: ***Lear, Macbeth***, and ***Hamlet***. The first of those societies is the truthful echo of the actual, morally depraved culture of Rome of that time in world history. The cultures of the latter three societies represented by Shakespeare, are also depraved and also frankly quite mad as well. It is *that quality of historical specificity* of the relevant culture, in each actual historical (Julius Caesar's Rome), or legendary case.

With those words, we have now entered a domain densely permeated by Classical forms of *irony*.

The language on stage is from Shakespeare's England, but that speech is used to convey an ancient culture which is not congruent with the use of the English prescribed by Shakespeare; for ***Julius Caesar***, it must be the actual, depraved Roman soul, using the English language for revealing the character of its true self at the time and place of the referenced events.[15] *Irony!* The principle is the same emphasis on accurate historical specificity which Shakespeare sought to convey in his account of the reign and fall of the Venetian-Norman tyranny's reign over the medieval history of England, this time applied to the historical case presented, and no other. *Irony!*

Incompetents such as the Romantic or Modernist, will stage these dramas as a costuming of action on stage which is not of the historic setting identified, but a poorly disguised reflection of contemporary English-speaking culture. Whereas, to underline the relevant, implied quality of contrast at issue here, it was pointed out to me that Schiller's poem ***The Cranes of Ibykus*** was crafted by Schiller through a rather exhaustive pre-crafting involving Goethe, Wilhelm von Humboldt, and others, with the intent to convey the richly ironical feeling of the language and mood of actual Corinth of

---

15. For reasons I develop a few paragraphs below, there is no fault in that use of English by either Shakespeare or the modern director.

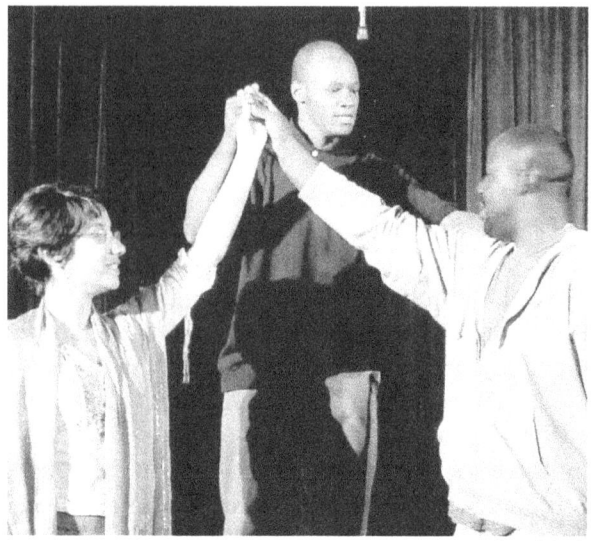
Gene Schenk

Sylvia Spaniolo

Members of the LaRouche Youth Movement in Los Angeles (left) performing Shakespeare's Julius Caesar, *under the direction of Robert Beltran and (right) working on Gauss's conformal mapping. "All serious Classical art, and its production, are, like true physical science, the process of building the better future in which our descendants will live. True science, like true art, has no more compelling commitment than this."*

the living Ibykus's actual time and place, but in Schiller's own German. A richness of *irony!*

It is of crucial importance for the benefit of the audience, that faithful attention, such as Schiller gave to his composition of **The Cranes of Ibykus**, be given to the intended historical-specificity. This, evokes a sense of eeriness, *irony*, which the competent staging of any of those dramas will evoke.

As Schiller emphasizes, the man from the street should leave the theater as virtually a different person than had entered a few hours before. *Irony!* This effect is not, like the experience of some fundamentalist parson's rant, some maudlin sort of edifying moral effect upon the audience. It is the effect on the citizen of looking over the shoulder of a history different than that of his own experience of life in his own time and place. *Irony!* "Why could they not see the rottenness of their culture? Could I do something about a tragic error in the culture of my own society today? What kind of a fool I would be, if I could not look at my own culture as I could now see so clearly the insanity of that other culture presented to me by that play?" *Irony!* He is not such a fool that he would attempt to deduce a principle for his culture from the other culture on stage.

The citizen's passion should not be mustered with the intent to change the history of that culture which pranced on stage, or to adduce a moral recipe from it; he must develop relevant insight into the qualitatively dif-

ferent historical specificities of his own culture. Only a weird sort of fool of a man would portray himself, on stage, or in life, as experiencing the condition of pregnancy. *Irony!*

We each dwell in a part of the larger fabric of history as a whole, in these cases, European history; the Earth is not flat, nor is any significant interval of culture in history. The culture of any place and interval has specific, dynamic characteristics, within, and with respect to differences with any larger portion of history. It is those differences—*ironies!*—which are the appropriate subject of the playwright's and director's attentions. The competent playwright, as Friedrich Schiller prescribes, is primarily an historian of a special distinction. Any Classical drama must be a voyage of the mind of the audience to some specific time and place in history, as it were a visit to a country where one's own language is, *ironically*, not actually spoken, and where habits of social interaction are *ironically* different. It is a sense of history from the vantage-point of this *ironical* quality of conscious experience of changes of quality of composition among cultures, among societies, among successive generations of even the same society, such as the typical qualitative cultural conflict between "Baby Boomers" and young, university-age adults today, which is the included subject of the broad mission of the Classical drama in general.

This brings us to the next quality to be considered.

Thus, whereas the Romantic or Existentialist sitting in the audience during the performance, imagines, in his or her simple-minded way, that he, or she, as a member of the audience is observing the behavior on stage, and is reacting to that which he, or she is witnessing: *On the contrary, the playwright, director, and actors are, ironically, observing the members of the audience, and drawing conclusions about the expected and actual performance by that audience, and also about themselves!* All is *irony!* I explain:

The orbit of the planets is not circular, but elliptical. *Irony!* Fermat demonstrated that the pathway of least action is not the shortest distance, but the pathway of the quickest time. *Irony!* Huyghens thought this pathway was defined by the cycloid; but Leibniz and Bernouilli demonstrated that it is the catenary-defined principle of the Leibniz calculus, the principle of universal least action. *Irony!*

All great playwrights, directors, and actors dealing with Classical artistry in drama and poetry have proceeded from nothing less than *a controlling intimation* of the essential immortality of the experienced, living human individual and his species.[16] *Irony!* The substance corresponding to even such a mere intimation has an ontological actuality corresponding to such examples as Bernhard Riemann's representation of the correct metaphysical apprehension of the notion of Dirichlet's Principle, as Riemann carries this beyond Dirichlet's own argument, in Riemann's work on Abelian functions: Abelian functions are the expression of, *literally, unbounded irony*, which is itself an ironical conception. On the correct use of the term "metaphysical," as I employ that term here, I refer the reader of these lines to the comparison provided in the essential argument which I supply as the kernel of my ***Vernadsky and Dirichlet's Principle***.

To repeat the core of that argument, I say the following here. In the scientifically correct use of the term *metaphysical*, science emphasizes the conditional validity of sense-experience, that it represents, at best, shadows of efficient reality, shadows which have been generated, as effects of the action of unsensed, but provably efficient principles upon the individual human being's sense-perceptual apparatus. Universal principles are never seen directly by the senses, but, at best, only the existence of their effects, as something undeniably efficient, but which, like the concepts of the mathematical physicists' complex domain, does not itself appear as an object of sense-perception.

What is real is not that which a naive reading of sense-impressions suggests, but, rather, that, at best, that which is not directly known to sense-impressions has produced as a shadow cast upon the sensorium. *That is the essence of irony! It is such irony which unites physical science and the practice of valid Classical artistic composition, as congruent features of human knowledge of man in the universe in which we exist.*

It is that principle of irony which is the true principle of all composition and performance of Classical art. It is that which unites all of the work of Leonardo da Vinci as a single enterprise.

To communicate that which is true, one must rely on the irony of the developmental process of constant change which merges the domains of the mortal and immortality into a single experience. That is the highest expression of Classical art. That is the indispensable function performed by Classical artistic composition and its performance.

Life as Art: The Principle of Tragedy

So, in the work of Vernadsky, life exists, provably, as a universal principle, but, as I emphasized in the indicated location, life can not be located functionally within the relatively universal domain of abiotic processes. It acts on, and acts within the bounds of the abiotic domain, but life as such is not part of that domain, and is above it. Similarly, the Noösphere is defined by a principle of cognition which can not be located within the confines of the domain of biology as such, and is above it. References to such physically efficient principles as those, are the only sane use of the term "metaphysical," just as the Gauss-Riemann conception of the complex domain identifies the ontologically metaphysical actuality of all experienced physical processes in the universe.

This notion of physically efficient metaphysical existence, was already understood by such ancients as the Pythagoreans and Plato. It appears in Platonic and Christian theology, for example, as the notion of the immortality of an individual human personality, as a quality of the personality whose function within the Noösphere is bounded by the existence of the living person, but whose distinctive existence, as a distinct human personality, is located within the realm of a principle which does not experience biological death. Thus, in the work of Vernadsky and his relevant predecessors,

---

16. On the record, even the English poet Wordsworth acknowledged the relevance of this topic, but without actually describing it efficiently.

only life as such can produce life, and *only the principle of individual cognition as such can produce cognition.*

Therefore, all truly sane persons, and societies, too, locate their primary sense of self-interest in the notion of immortality associated with the existence of human life within the Noösphere, if only as *an intimation of immortality*. The only rational use of the term "Classical" in European civilization today dates, to our best present knowledge, from such exponents of this persuasion as the Pythagoreans and Plato, and, implicitly, to their tracing of such conceptions to earlier developments within Egyptian civilization. All European Classical science and art are subjects of that view of the nature of the individual member of mankind in the universe.

Take Shakespeare's work, for example.

For the England of Christopher Marlowe and Shakespeare, since the relevant pack of Venetian scallywags—such as Zorzi ("Giorgi"), Cardinal Pole, Thomas Cromwell, et al.—had effected the judicial murder of Sir Thomas More, their modern England had taken on attributes of a horrid Venetian nightmare. The earlier liberation of England, led by Richmond (Henry VII), had launched an England which had been freed so from the long tyranny of the *ultramontane* forces of the Venetian-Norman partnership, and had been a blessing: the experience of the modern sovereign commonwealth. This commonwealth of Sir Thomas More's time was now gravely endangered, as, again, later, during Shakespeare's time, menaced by the emergence of a New Party of Venice in a late-Sixteenth-Century England becoming dominated, more and more, by the figure of Paolo Sarpi and such emerging prominent Sarpi agents of the early Seventeenth Century as the depraved Sir Francis Bacon and Thomas Hobbes.

For such as Shakespeare's circle of followers of Sir Thomas More, et al., there would have been no Richmond but for France's Louis XI, and no reign of Louis but for Jeanne d'Arc. That history reached back to deep layers of humanity, long before the evil which had been imperial Rome. Under the influence of such followers of Paolo Sarpi as Bacon, Hobbes, and John Locke, Shakespeare's plays were either banned, or mangled and virtually destroyed by their producers, until their legacy was rescued from a British intellectual sewer by the circles of such German founders of the late Eighteenth-Century Classical insurgency of such admirers of Shakespeare's original work as Abraham Kästner, Kästner's student Gotthold Lessing,

Moses Mendelssohn, Goethe, and Schiller.[17]

On the Classical stage, human history is immortal in that way, dwelling forever within a "simultaneity of eternity" as Raphael Sanzio portrays this in the Vatican Museum's *School of Athens*. It is on that stage in mankind's eternity, that the Classical drama situates both the play and its audience, just as the Aeschylus of *Prometheus Bound* situates Prometheus and mankind in the immortal struggle against the evil, implicitly satanic tyranny of the Olympian Zeus. Compare Shakespeare's treatment of Hamlet with a certain characteristic of Aeschylus' *Prometheus Bound*, and with the attempt by P.B. Shelley to reconstruct it.

The prevalent fault in ancient Greek tragedy, prior to Aeschylus' *Prometheus* trilogy and Plato's related protest against the tragedians generally, is the lack of even a prescience of an *ironically posed shadow of a remedy for the future society*, in the drama: Schiller's "Sublime." *Prometheus Bound* is an exception to this deficiency in Classical tragedy before Plato. In the accounts of the trilogy which have been supplied, Prometheus is freed from captivity and torment in the concluding, third part of that drama. Therein lies the awesome power arrayed against Zeus, a power which was already ironically implicit in the preceding *Prometheus Bound*.

In that instance, the remedy is found, not within the drama misread as the interpretation of a script. The solution lies in the mind of the audience, in that they are human, and are watching mankind's benefactor being tortured for reason of his defense of the right of human beings (of which the audience is, ironically, largely composed) to express their natural aptitude for discovering and employing beneficial universal principles. Those who remember Solon of Athens' letter to his dec-

---

17. Abraham Kästner (1719-1800) was a leading mathematician of Eighteenth-Century Germany, a principal teacher and later collaborator of Gotthold Lessing, one of the two principal teachers of Carl F. Gauss, with E.A.W. Zimmerman, a one-time host of Benjamin Franklin, and a key part of the circle which brought the anti-Locke influence of Leibniz's **New Essays on Human Understanding** into the leading position it occupies in the crafting of the 1776 U.S. Declaration of Independence. Kästner played a key role in the revival of the actual work of Shakespeare in and from Germany. However, after Carl F. Gauss's 1799 doctoral dissertation, attacking the hoaxes of D'Alembert, Euler, and Lagrange, the empiricist school of Gauss and Riemann's Nineteenth-Century and later adversaries, has sought to defame Kästner, and send his memory into obscurity. It was the launching of the Eighteenth-Century German Classic by these circles, which brought the Classical legacy of Shakespeare back into that English-speaking part of the world associated with Benjamin Franklin and Percy B. Shelley. *Irony!*

adent fellow-citizens of that earlier occasion, have the implied capacity to recognize that the persecuted Prometheus is their benefactor being persecuted on their own account. The drama, the **Prometheus Bound** portion of the trilogy, has Constitutional implications of a quality reflected in the founding of our U.S. republic. The section from Goethe's fragmentary **Grosskopta** in which the character Prometheus curses Zeus, is a relevant reference on this point.[18] Such irony is the secret of all the Classical poetry and drama, as composed and performed, still worthy of our attention today!

The Olympian myth expresses a condition of society in which a reigning oligarchy has reduced the conditions of life of the majority of humanity to those of wild, or tamed human cattle. Such cattle are forbidden to employ, or even to imagine the discovery of universal physical principles, such as what is portrayed in the play as the use of fire. Their knowledge of means by which the human condition of the generality of the people must be improved, is forbidden. This is called, euphemistically, the "traditional culture" prescribed for human cattle; therefore, the killing of the human slave who has acquired literacy, that done by the hand of the beast which writes the laws.

To follow Shakespeare's work properly, we must take this principle of that Aeschylus play into account: in Hamlet, for example. As Shakespeare puts the point in the character Horatio's aside to the audience, in the closing scene of the play, we must learn the lesson of the preceding events which have occurred, not in England, but on stage, lest we repeat their equal in the future. This is not said to the Scandinavian population of the drama, but, rather, to the English audience present at the performance of the play. The playing of the play itself is, on that occasion, the triumph of the author, players, and audience, over the evil which is Hamlet's rotten state of Denmark. There is no "happy ending" within that drama itself, but, access to a happy outcome for some present, or future audience which is adequately inspired by the irony of the drama they have experienced.

Thus, in both Aeschylus' **Prometheus**, or the dramas of the matured Shakespeare, Lessing, and Schiller, and the best work of Goethe, the sheer awfulness of a terrible culture is used as a springboard for foreseeing what Schiller defines as the principle of *the Sublime*. The individual person must be greater than his, or her personal destiny. Aeschylus' **Prometheus** typifies that issue, as did both the real-life Jeanne d'Arc and Schiller's truthful presentation of her on stage. All Classical European drama is subject to that standard for defining its purpose and its essence.

There is no mortal "happy ending" within the real-life drama of Jeanne d'Arc as an individual; there is her actual immortality, in the self-liberation from Norman tyranny of a France inspired by her mission. She has died, as all men and women will die by one means or another; but, she has achieved immortality, *ironically*, through the manner in which she dealt with the peril which overtook her mortal existence.

The case of Shakespeare's **Richard III** brings the issue of the real-life Jeanne d'Arc into sharp focus, as Schiller does with his play.

Despite the Classical conception of man expressed within the best moments of ancient Greek culture, such as the letter of Solon of Athens, or the doctrines of immortality and *agapē* presented by Plato, the condition of the people generally was their subjugation to a state of relative bestiality, as virtually human cattle herded by oligarchies like that of the mythical Gods of Olympus. The moral degeneration of Athens, by forms of reductionist philosophy verging from the Eleatics and others into Sophistry, the rise of the evil which was the Roman Empire, the Byzantine empire, and the *ultramontane* tyranny managed by the alliance of Venice's financier oligarchy and the Norman chivalry, present us a long history of anguish, an extended tragedy. Finally, in the Fifteenth-Century Renaissance, a new form of society was established on the basis of the principle of *agapē*: the commonwealths of Louis XI's France and Henry VII's England, a new condition of mankind in modern Europe, a better condition spawned by the great Renaissance of that century.

True art addresses nothing less than subjects of kindred grandeur of spiritual capacity for good, or, failing that, for evil. Shakespeare's **Richard III** must be seen, with Richmond's virtual slaying of the old dragon of Norman chivalry, as the liberation of mankind from an ancient great evil, as the justification of the suffering of the Christian martyrs under Roman imperial oppression, from Nero to Diocletian, and as the horror which the partnership of Venetian financier oligarchy and Norman chivalry had produced as the virtually geno-

---

18. This was set as a song by Hugo Wolf. The Hugo Wolf Society's recorded performance by the famous bass and cantor Friedrich Schorr, is a notable reference—in spite of my objections to much of Wolf's work and critical opinions otherwise.

cidal New Dark Age of Europe's Fourteenth Century.

From great Classical tragedy the member of the audience obtains nothing so much as an intimation of immortality, the immortality of the actual Jeanne d'Arc whom Schiller brings to life, by aid of Classical dramatic devices, on the stage. Or, the real-life meaning of the mission of the Rev. Martin Luther King. The object to be grasped is the immortal meaning of one's own brief, mortal existence. The question to be posed is, "What shall I do with this mortal life which will fulfill the mission of this brief mortal existence?" That is the ironical difference between human life and the awful littleness of soul expressed in Lord Chesterfield's famous collection of letters, or the misreading of Classical drama which becomes a collection of relatively petty moralizing in the Romantic's or existentialist's smothering of the presentation of a Classical drama or poetry.

The meaning of the mortal individual human life is located in the future of society. "What, dear fellow, might be the immortal purpose for which you are living as a mortal being today?" The sense of Classical tragedy impels us to hear the anguish of the past, its unrealized achievements, and to discover, if we are able to do so, the means for nourishing an outcome which the past has consigned to realization in either our present, or our future. Serious citizens think several generations, or even more, ahead. They do so not by indulging in wild fantasies, but in selecting some cornerstones to be laid today, which are a necessary step toward something of importance to humanity to be realized in the future. So, as an economist of my years, I make no policy which does not look forward to a world of today's young adults, a world of their experience a half-century—two generations—yet to come.

All great art is great precisely to the degree it expresses that kind of intention underlying the relevant action of the artist. Such is the nature, purpose, and required quality of performance of Classical tragedy and poetry. All serious Classical art, and its production, are, like true physical science, the process of building the better future in which our descendants will live. True science, like true art, has no more compelling commitment than this. So, Classical drama and poetry must be understood, and produced.

In the immortality of human souls, all find justice, the good and the evil alike, and the cowardly and merely useless, too. Such is the nature of competent science.

2. Economy As Humanism

A foolish economist measures the performance of an economy in the financial, or monetary, or, much less foolishly, the physical wealth enjoyed by either some, or all of the members of that society. The competent economist measures the wealth of the economy in the degree of self-improvement of the quality of the members of society as human. Making the same point more bluntly, it were said that the economic mission of society is to make the nation's people better than they are today. This is to be done through means employing the process of developing the people to higher levels of power in and over nature per capita. Or, we might better say, "The greatest wealth which the generation of the deceased has bequeathed to its heirs, is a society of a better quality of living people."

The opposing, popular, but wicked point of view of most contemporary courses of instruction in economics, measures wealth as Adam Smith did in an ugly, relevant passage within his notorious 1759 **Theory of the Moral Sentiments,** which I have quoted on several occasions:

"The administration of the great system of the universe ... the care of the universal happiness of all rational and sensible beings, is the business of God and not of man. To man is allotted a much humbler department, but one more suitable to the weakness of his powers, and to the narrowness of his comprehension; the care of his family, his friends, his country.... But, though we are ... endowed with a very strong desire of those ends, it has been intrusted to the slow and uncertain determinations of our reason to find out the proper means of bringing them about. *Nature has directed us to the greater part of these by original and immediate instincts. Hunger, thirst, the passion which unites the two sexes, the love of pleasure, and the dread of pain, prompt us to apply these means for their own sake, and without any consideration of their tendency to those beneficent ends which the great Director of nature intended to produce by them.*"[19]

It was this book by Smith which should be recognized by relevant scholars and economists as a significant part of the background for Lord Shelburne's 1763 assignment of the same Adam Smith, to undertake tasks

19. Cf. Lyndon H. LaRouche, Jr., with David P. Goldman, et al., **The Ugly Truth About Milton Friedman** (New York: New Benjamin Franklin House, 1980), p. 107. Emphasis added here by LaRouche.

of subversive operations against both France and the English colonies in North America. In carrying out that assigned mission, Smith followed faithfully the doctrine of promotion of private vices of the pro-Satanic Bernard Mandeville of *The Fable of the Bees* notoriety. Smith generously plagiarized the Physiocrats Dr. François Quesnay and Turgot in producing his 1776 attack, known by the short title of *The Wealth of Nations*, on the founding of the United States of America.

By virtue of breeding, the East India Company's Shelburne preferred the methods of the Venetian stiletto, to the costlier enterprise of frontal bayonet charges. Thus, this was the same Lord Shelburne who used as a stiletto his notorious Martinist freemasonic order associated with the circles of Voltaire, of such as Jacques Necker, the Duke of Orléans, Count Cagliostro, Casanova, et al. which conducted the series of operations used to destabilize and overthrow the French government, through stunts such as the affair of the Queen's Necklace. It was this same Martinist stiletto which used Shelburne's British Foreign Office of his dirty-operations specialist Jeremy Bentham to launch the terrorist activities of the London-trained British agents Danton and Marat, and later Robespierre.

That was the same Martinist order, under the leadership of that Count Joseph de Maistre who crafted the personality designed for, and adopted by Napoleon Bonaparte for the latter's transformation from a Robespierre asset into the great monster whose wars, by 1815, had created a situation of subsequently ricocheting effects, from which continental Europe has never fully recovered, to the present day. Indeed, Joseph de Maistre's design for what became known later as the Napoleonic imperial model used under the rubric of *Synarchism*, was the basis for the launching and continuing deployment of the European financier-created model of Mussolini and Hitler, including the de Maistre-prompted persecution and mass-murder of Jews by the Nazi dictatorships during the 1922-1945 post-Versailles Treaty interval.

www.clipart.com

Lord Shelburne (1737-1805) of the British Foreign Office "preferred the methods of the Venetian stiletto to the costlier enterprise of frontal bayonet charges. Thus he used Adam Smith and the Martinists to launch subversive operations against both France and the English colonies in North America."

The net result of that brutish ideology represented by Shelburne's Adam Smith, has been the British-monarchy-sponsored myths of *both* capitalism and Marx's socialism.

The U.S. Constitutional system was never either a capitalist or socialist "economic model." It was only to the degree that European nations, such as Bismarck's Germany and Alexander II's Russia, adopted the counsel of American System economist Henry C. Carey, that continental Europe has rivalled the United States in the field of physical economy. It was always the American System of political-economy which guided President Franklin Roosevelt's transformation of an economy wrecked under Andrew Mellon-controlled Presidents Coolidge and Hoover, into the most powerful economy the world had ever seen, the same economy successfully ruined during the past three decades under policies more radically destructive than anything experienced under Mellon and Hoover.

In contrast to contemporary European constitutions and systems, *the actual form of society which the U.S. Declaration of Independence and Federal Constitution, with its crucial Preamble, define the U.S. economy to be, is neither capitalism nor socialism, but what U.S. Treasury Secretary Alexander Hamilton, among others, defined as The American System of political-economy.* What the British system, and the Karl Marx it trained, defined as "capitalism," was the British imperial form of Anglo-Dutch, Venetian-style *ultramontane* rule by a financier oligarchy. This was the system established by the victory of the Anglo-Dutch financier oligarchy, centered in the power obtained by the British East India Company through the February 1763 Treaty of Paris, which concluded the preceding, mutually ruinous "Seven Years War" among the powers of continental Europe.[20] From 1848 on, the power of the old feudal systems of Europe, such as those of the decadent Habsburgs,

---

20. The precedent for the British imperial monarchy's orchestration, under Prince of Wales and later King Edward VII, of the mutual ruin of continental Europe through World War I.

were largely absorbed in what became, increasingly, the appendages of the Anglo-Dutch Liberal monarchical system.[21] The power in this imperial system was located in that financier oligarchy which became known as the *Synarchist International* of the Twentieth Century, the same Synarchist International whose cabal of private bankers gave us Mussolini, Hitler, and World War II.

The European system, which credulous of the world have accepted as what they describe as "the capitalist system," is, in fact, usually the system of tyrannical rule which the private financier-oligarchical syndicates of Europe and elsewhere have exerted as a power placed legally above the authority of governments, through arrangements often described today as "independent central-banking systems." The present European Central Bank is a version of this. It was that arrangement, consolidated during the Versailles Treaty proceedings following World War I, which gave the world the Bank of England's one-time choice Adolf Hitler and all the evil which he came to represent.[22] It is that same cabal, in its present form, which has brought the world now into a collapse far more menacing than that of 1929-1931, to the verge of an intrinsically bankrupt system of "globalization" which would lead the planet as a whole into a prolonged new dark age.

There have been serious attempts at establishing Presidential systems in Europe consistent with the U.S. model, as the attempts of de Gaulle under the Fifth Republic attest. However, as soon as the superior authority of some "independent central banking" system as a superior national, or international authority, is usually affirmed, the sovereignty of the nation becomes merely conditional upon the continued pleasure of the true ruling power, the reigning financier oligarchy.

The relevant point of formal confusion in opinions concerning the comparison of the American System to its usual European rivals, has been the fact that the American System does use the notion of price, and profit on sales of priced goods, as the medium within which private entrepreneurship functions. The difference in principle becomes clear once we simply put aside the notion of capitalism as the British system defines it, and replace that with the American System of political-economy. This difference is blurred only to the degree that American practice is corrupted to significant degree by the influence of the Europe-designed international financial-oligarchical power.

The essential difference, especially so when the discussion of economy is situated within the framework of culture as treated in the preceding section of this report, is that the British system is essentially, as Germany's Chancellor has recently observed, an intrinsically *amoral* system, based in fact upon the supremacy of financial usury;[23] whereas the American System of political-economy is premised upon pervasive, controlling universal types of moral considerations, upheld by those Germans and other Europeans who share belief in the higher authority of our own Constitutional principle of promotion of the general welfare, which Plato and the Christian Apostle Paul defined as *agapē*. These are the considerations implied in the opening paragraph of this present chapter.

Modern Society

The clear dividing-line between medieval and modern European civilization is the impact of the process associated with the Fifteenth Century's great ecumenical Council of Florence. The U.S. Federal Constitution of 1789 is the heir of the revolution in principles of government established by that Council. The most typical of the writings defining the functional meaning of that distinction, are two works of (Cardinal) Nicholas of Cusa: his **Concordantia Catholica**, superseding Dante Alighieri's **De Monarchia** as a definition of the founding of the modern sovereign form of nation-state republic; and his launching of modern experimental science with a series of works beginning with his **De Docta Ignorantia**, and including his proposal for what became Christopher Columbus's voyages of discovery to North and Central America.

Admittedly, this Council did not establish a prescribed form of the modern state, but, rather, specified the ecumenical principles already implicit in Christianity under which the organization of peoples among sov-

---

21. Thus the former feudalistic aristocracy of Europe and beyond was chiefly absorbed into the role of subordinates, even mere lackeys, of the "bourgeois" monarchies of Britain and the Netherlands.

22. The chief instrument coordinating Hitler's rise to power was the Bank of England's Montagu Norman, whose most notable agent in this matter was banker Hjalmar Schacht. It was the German-Soviet negotiations leading toward an initial Nazi attack westward, rather than eastward, which spun some among the relevant financier circles which had brought Mussolini and Hitler into power, into a temporary commitment to destroy Hitler, before returning to deploy on behalf of fascist-like perspectives as soon as President Franklin Roosevelt was dead.

23. The principle of usury has been defended against the Preamble of the U.S. Federal Constitution among some U.S. circles such as Associate Justice Antonin Scalia, defended as the same Lockean doctrine of "shareholder value" which was banned by the Declaration of Independence and Preamble of the Federal Constitution, but which was the argument made by the advocates of chattel slavery prior to 1861-1865.

"The clear dividing line between medieval and modern European civilization is the impact of the process associated with the Fifteenth Century's great ecumenical Council of Florence...." Here, a detail from Benozzo Gozzoli's "Journey of the Magi," depicting the arrival at the Council of a delegation of religious leaders, poets, philosophers, and statesmen.

across the Atlantic and to Asian destinations, became a long-ranging policy, as by Christopher Columbus and Sir Thomas More's England, to establish allies for these policies of the great Council in more distant regions of the planet. The combined effect of the efforts in this direction, resulted in the establishment of a system of sovereign nation-states in the Americas, including the emergence of the U.S.A. as the first modern nation-state with a refined design expressing the best knowledge of all known parts of European civilization up to that time.

The U.S.A. was built by Europeans. As the case of the founding and early, pre-1688 development of the Massachusetts Bay Colony attests, the U.S.A. was not the outcome of a blind flight of refugees from Europe, although many did come as refugees. We were built, as the case of the Seventeenth-Century Massachusetts Bay Colony attests, to establish on our shores a kind of republic which could not be created within Europe under the conditions of the efforts of the European financiers and other oligarchs to crush the achievements of the Fifteenth-Century Renaissance with the weapon of religious warfare.

With the British Foreign Office's orchestration of what became known as the Martinist order's French Revolutions of 1789-1815, we knew, as the policies of Secretary of State John Quincy Adams attest to this, that we could not survive as a nation, in face of threats of our destruction from locations such as London's and Metternich's Europe, unless we built our republic to a level of sufficient strength to defend itself against these bloody adversaries. To that end, Adams virtually created a functioning form of our Department of State, with its presently continuing tradition of a system of well-informed, thinking historians, and coupled this effort with clearly defined territorial objectives. We defined the U.S.A. thus as a continental power, a sover-

ereign states might be arranged. However, the results of the findings by the Council were soon realized as the first modern European sovereign nation-states committed to the principle of *agapē*.

The included outcome of these proposed reforms was the founding of the form of modern nation-state known as the *commonwealth,* which was first established in Louis XI's France, and then Henry VII's England. This notion of the principle of the commonwealth was affirmed in the first provision of the agreement to end religious warfare with which the 1648 Treaty of Westphalia opens, as presented in a more perfect way in the 1776 U.S. Declaration of Independence and 1789 Federal Constitution. The concept of "promote the general welfare," as an integral feature of the supreme principle of Constitutional law in the Preamble of the Constitution, is an expression of the qualitative distinction, on principle, between the European cultures' forms of feudal and modern society.

To assess the history of modern European civilization since those modern developments, we must fairly say that Cardinal Nicholas of Cusa's prophetic perspective for reaching out from Europe through voyages eign republic between its intended permanent northern and southern borders and from the Atlantic to the Pacific oceans. With President Lincoln's victory against the London-orchestrated pro-slavery revolt of 1861-1865, we became a powerful nation by assimilating floods of then chiefly European immigrants to settle and develop the territory of our republic.

To the degree we afforded these immigrants the opportunities to freely develop their cultural and productive potentials, these immigrants contributed to the U.S.A. what they would not have been permitted to accomplish in Europe. Thus, through policies typified by those of Presidents Lincoln and Franklin Roosevelt, the U.S.A. became the first true modern European republic, a republic premised upon a Constitution rooted in a distillation of the greatest achievements produced by European civilization up to that time.

"The U.S.A. was built by Europeans." The principles of the commonwealth and promoting the general welfare, affirmed by the Council of Florence (1431-1445), were the inspirations for the U.S. Declaration of Independence and the 1789 Federal Constitution, Here, George Washington presiding over the 1789 Constitutional Convention, as depicted by Howard Chandler Christy.

Once we had achieved that much, President Franklin Roosevelt pointed us toward a still broader objective, of extending the benefits of what we had accomplished thus far, to not only the American republics beyond our borders, but to establish a concordant relationship with the existing or emerging nations of Eurasia, Africa, Australia, AND New Zealand. That intention was largely aborted under that President's successor, but it remains the proper long-range strategic outlook for the U.S.A. today.

Now, that much said of modern political history as background, proceed to the principal subject of this chapter of the report. Now, go directly to the point of the paragraph with which I opened this chapter.

I wrote: "…The competent economist measures the wealth of the economy in the degree of self-improvement of the quality of the members of society as human…. [W]e might say, 'The greatest wealth which the generation of the deceased has bequeathed to its heirs, is a society of a better quality of living people.'" With that, we turn to a matter in which the principle of irony is carried to a higher, but already implied form.

Since mankind is a higher quality of existence than life itself otherwise, what, we might ask, is the natural self-interest of humanity, beyond the reach of mere biology as such? What, consequently, is the natural self-

interest of the human individual? Must that natural self-interest not be an expression of that which sets the existence of the human individual apart from, as above the mere biological existence of the individual and his, or her species?

Focus upon a finer point subsumed within that argument. *Since this distinction of the human species is located, in action, only in those creative-mental powers which exist only as the sovereign activity of the individual human mind, what is the universal purpose for the existence of that individual?*

Since the individual expresses this unique quality, associated with Vernadsky's physical-scientific definition of the existence of the Noösphere, the only immortal purpose of human existence is the expression of that specific kind of individual sovereignty.

However, this sovereign function of the individual is not circumscribed by his or her individual creations; it includes the maintaining of the immortality of that same quality expressed by others. This means, the responsibility of the living individual to absorb, and thus preserve the discoveries of principle by others, discoveries of principle to be embodied in the knowledgeable practice of future generations.

This also means the responsibility for nurturing the physical preconditions for practice of such knowledge by present and future society as a whole.

The notion of man as a sovereign immortal being

beyond his mere biological form, is defined thus. *That is the historically defined location of all human existence.*

Do they teach actual history, so, in your children's schools? If not, can you honestly say that your child is really being educated as a human being, rather than a human caricature of someone's pet puppy? Are you really qualified to provide your child the kind of home-schooling in history, and the history of science, required of a true human being, education for immortality? Is the child's public education much better than that? *Is that child undergoing the experience of actually discovering those ideas which have the distinctly human quality of irony to which I have referred in the preceding chapter here?*

Look at the set of questions implied by arguments of that type from the vantage-point of our society's past and present physical economy.

Modern Economy

We may regard the evidence of the history of mankind's physical economies in two alternate ways. One, we may think of modern living mankind in terms of his or her viewing an accumulation of artefacts left as fossils of a quality specific to the Noösphere. Or, we may change to different point of view, to a three-part picture: 1.) Physical fossils of the Noösphere as such; 2.) Intellectual fossils passed down as an accumulation of surviving knowledge; and 3.) New discoveries of principles of Classical art and science as I have attacked this problem in the preceding chapter of this report. Looking at modern economy in the first way, is consistent with the currently more popular outlook on economy; looking at modern economy in the corrected, second way, in which we consider the society's acquired knowledge of physical principles, to date, as a higher kind of fossil, is the only properly acceptable way of thinking, the kind of thinking typified by modern thinkers such as Kepler, Leibniz, and Riemann, which should be considered acceptable to the principled humanist.

The policies associated with today's practice of so-called "globalization," have an established record as the intentional destruction of civilization, the intentional lowering of the standard of living of the human being, from the present level of more than six billions population, to return to a level of substantially less than one billion, which was typical of periods prior to the rise of modern European civilization. Part of this genocidal implication of "globalization" is the loss of physical improvements of the type of basic economic infrastructure. Part is the loss of the social-intellectual infrastructure which was built up under modern European civilization

as a legacy of such earlier sources as the Classical Greek heritage of the Pythagoreans, Solon of Athens, and Plato. The third, and most crucial loss, is the loss of morality typified by the neo-Malthusian ideologies associated with the impact of the U.S.-based Congress for Cultural Freedom.[24] The very idea of progress, on which all of the achievements of European civilization to date have depended, the will to be actually human, has been subverted with already disastrous effects, even globally.

Consider the effect of a shift in point of view of humanity today, from the two-point standard of merely physical fossils as such, and man, to the three-point standard of reference, of physical fossils, and intellectual fossils in the form of both discoveries of universal physical principle and of Classical artistry, both in relationship to the living, creatively thinking individual. Think of man existing within a simultaneity of eternity, in which the past is continuing to act on the present, to thus produce the future. *The most significant expression of the impact of the past upon the present and future, is the impact of the present generations' experiencing past discoveries in universal physical principle and in Classical artistic composition, as the way in which the future generations are produced.*

The latter action, within a simultaneity of eternity so defined, is the true determinant of value, *as a process of becoming, rather than a completed effect of the present moment to date.*

This is the point of entry into a domain of the greatest irony of them all, that we are being acted upon, and acting efficiently on the future in this way. This is the irony of acting now to become better than we are now, but, while, at the same time, acting through the improvement of infrastructure, of technology of production, and through Classical artistic composition, to act efficiently upon the future of the universe, even long after we are mortally dead. This is the true standard by which the measurements of the economists are to be measured, the standard of producing more powerful human beings in a universe better suited to the habitation of such persons.

So, finally, Classical science and Classical art represent the process of production of improved human beings, beings of increasing moral, as much as physical power, in and over the parts of the universe which our species inhabits. To become truly human, we must learn to think, thus, ironically.

---

24. Better named, since existentialist 1968, as "The Congress for Cultural Fornication."